Finger Lakes Feast

Central New York is having a golden culinary moment, with an abundance of home cooks and restaurant chefs who know how to coax the best from the local cheese, produce, and fish.

—*The New York Times*

Finger Lakes Feast

110 Delicious Recipes from New York's Hotspot for Wholesome Local Foods

Kate Harvey & Karl Zinsmeister

with photos by

Noah Zinsmeister

McBooks Press

Ithaca, NY

www.mcbooks.com

Published by McBooks Press 2012
Copyright © 2012 Kate Harvey and Karl Zinsmeister

Cover photos and, unless noted below, interior photos © 2012 Noah Zinsmeister.

Dust jacket and book design by Panda Musgrove.

Deer photo on page 89 © Carl Patrick, Seneca White Deer Inc.
Dinosaur Bar-B-Que photo on page 100 © 2012 Dinosaur Bar-B-Que
Wegmans' barn photo on page 76 © 2011 Wegmans

Additional photos—listed by page number—© Shutterstock.com: 27, Robyn Mackenzie; 37, Dennis Donohue; 46, Azurita; 59, Olegusk; 68, BARRI; 69, crolique; 85 (bottom), Olga Bogatyrenko; 91, Stephanie Frey; 96, intoit; 97, Catherine Murray; 108, Digivic; 112, grintan; 124, Dariusz Gora; 125, Jorge Moro; 131, marekuliasz; 146, Local Favorite Photography; 156–7, Colin D. Young; 179, Vania Georgieva; 182, Brett Rabideau.

Library of Congress Control Number: 2012947485

Visit the McBooks Press website at www.mcbooks.com.

Printed in the United States of America
9 8 7 6 5 4 3 2 1

To our family's bread makers, pie rollers, peach canners,
and creators of daily feasts—
who have taught, fed, inspired, and loved us always.

Table of Contents

Salads & Side Dishes   105

Sweets 147

Contributing Finger Lakes Restaurants 185

Resources 189

Creators 197

Index 199

Introduction

Why the Buzz about Finger Lakes Food?

The Finger Lakes region of Upstate New York—the highly scenic landscape of rolling farmland, forest, and deep lakes that inspired this cookbook and provided its many recipes—has followed a classic pattern observed in many locales across the globe as they became renowned for great food.

Very often, it begins with wine. Once good wine starts to emerge from a region, tastemakers commence visiting. Soon great chefs move in. As they sprinkle restaurants amidst the farm vineyards, a third shift takes place: a whole infrastructure springs up in support of fresh handmade food.

Local farmers start to grow fancy fruits and heirloom vegetables. Grass-fed beef, henhouses, and lambing operations commence to appear. Butchers learn to handle uncommon meats like goat, and they find new buyers for wild game. If the place is blessed with deep clear water and abundant game fish (as the Finger Lakes region emphatically is), fishermen start to smoke and sell their catches, and local hunters and pig farmers erect smokehouses of their own.

New York's Finger Lakes area is one of the most exciting and fastest-growing culinary hot spots in America today.

—Edible Finger Lakes

Eventually new demand arises for stone grinding of grains, for unusual vegetable oils, for distilleries. Small-batch cheese makers set up shop. Foragers find ready markets for special mushrooms, wild ginger, dandelion greens, ramps, cresses, and even milkweed buds they pluck from local forests and fields. Unusual creams and yogurts and other dairy specialties become available.

Orchards, grape yards, and berry patches sell more, better, and more varied fruit, and end up planting new acreage. Markets develop for less common crops and products such as buckwheat, antique tomatoes and beans, crème fraîche, and gooseberries. High-tech hydroponic vegetable production gets a foothold. Cottage industries begin to churn out exceptional honey, maple syrup, fruit butters, and sausages. Craft bakers and chocolatiers go into business.

Fine restaurants help catalyze these new efforts, but the newer, tastier, fresher products quickly become a normal part of the local food stream. That certainly has been the case in the Finger Lakes region as it has climbed rapidly into one of our country's centers for excellent and interesting eating. While the four million food and wine tourists who visit every year are an important stimulus to the area's culinary boom, the largest portion of the regional food web serves nearby residents.

The Finger Lakes continues its rapid transition into one of America's signature wine and food regions.

—Syracuse Post-Standard

There are legions of enthusiastic customers for the bounty generated on the more than two million acres of dedicated farmland in central New York. By our count, there are now at least 71 local farmer's markets, 156 U-pick farms, and 45 separate farms offering CSAs (community-supported agriculture) to subscribers who receive weekly "shares" of a farm's fruits and vegetables throughout the growing season. At least five local-food distribution networks (for example, Regional Access) have sprung up solely to supply regionally sourced food to area consumers, restaurants, and institutions. There are scads of excellent newsletters, many local-food groups, and good food writers at regional publications.

In addition to snapping up the area's superb agricultural raw materials, locals and visitors patronize lots of skilled chefs. The small city of Ithaca, in the heart of the Finger Lakes, has more restaurants per capita than New York City. Other parts of the region are close behind. Many superior restaurants serve first-rate, often unusual, food—generally with a heavy reliance on local ingredients.

To produce this cookbook, we collaborated with more than two dozen of the very best chefs in the Finger Lakes. We also picked the brains and recipe files of many of the most intriguing farmers, food artisans, and vendors, plus some long-time residents. Many of these favorite recipes are inspired by great nearby food sources, or are specialties of the area.

You will find some exquisite gourmet food in these pages. You will also discover plenty of refreshing simple dishes. And in-between you'll encounter lots of delicious, wholesome, very comfortable cooking and eating.

We've added many explanatory asides, some quirky local history, and detailed source information to help you enjoy what you're eating (and later find more of it in stores or online). We photographed most of the dishes as they emerged from our test kitchen, to give you a clearer sense of the food.

We also included shots of local scenes encountered during our research to offer a glimpse into the region that created these wondrous edibles. Should you develop wanderlust and wish to indulge in a little food travel or agritourism, you'll find lots of tips here on places where you can stimulate your eyes and taste buds.

It all begins in ice. When the last glaciers retreated from Upstate New York about 10,000 years ago, they left behind a landscape of deep crystalline lakes, steep hillsides, and dramatic gorges. There was plenty of rich land, but for the first two centuries of U.S. history there were no settlers—because central and western New York were the homeland of the Iroquois, the most rooted and vigilant Indians on the continent.

The six tribes of the Iroquois Confederacy hunted the forests and cultivated corn, beans, squash, and orchard fruits across Upstate New York. Iroquois braves jealously watched the rivers and footpaths, so the area remained wild more than a century after New York City, Boston, and Philadelphia had become crowded metropolises.

During the American Revolution the Iroquois sided with the British, and after the war most of them relocated to Canada. Hardy American farmers started to plant the region that had been the Iroquois homeland, quickly making it a breadbasket for the nation. The opening of the Erie Canal a few decades later brought a population boom, as well as great economic and cultural dynamism. The area bubbled with utopian fervor and religious innovation. Abolitionism, temperance, women's rights, and other social causes were born here. Educational, political, and artistic reforms poured out of the region.

The American Arts & Crafts Movement and the Craftsman home wave that swept America during the early 1900s were centered in central and western New York. Gustav Stickley, Harvey Ellis, Adelaide Robineau, Elbert Hubbard, and other residents democratized art and beautified the ways everyday Americans lived at home. They celebrated natural simplicity as a route to human happiness.

They did all this in highly entrepreneurial ways. While the Arts & Crafts Movement in Europe was linked to rage against machines and suspicion of capitalism, the version flowing out of Upstate New York embraced technology as a way to reduce drudgery and elevate quality. The Stickley brothers celebrated new commercial techniques such as direct-to-consumer sales and home production as ways to make the good life available and affordable to everyday citizens.

Today's culinary bloom in the Finger Lakes is taking place in very much that same democratic mold. Whereas in many regions, exceptionally good food and drink have become costly—and pompous—indulgences, the Finger Lakes spirit is to make good eating casual, simple, unintimidating, and relatively inexpensive.

The restaurants are never stiff or starchy. Many of the chefs wander among the tables. Farmers and producers deal directly and closely with their customers. It's an enormously fun place to explore the craft of food.

This region has emerged as the most important enological and culinary destination in the Eastern United States.

—food writer Michael Turback

Even the wineries are welcoming and relaxed in the Finger Lakes. Most are family owned and located right on the farm where the grapes are grown. (New York isn't dominated by giant winemaking corporations like California and Washington are.)

Most wineries will let you taste their wares for a fee in the range of $2–$5. (Estates in California and Europe can charge up to $40 for tastings.) And winery staff are approachable and friendly. Along with your five or six samples, you'll generally get lots of information, with no attitude. If you'd like to buy a bottle, you'll find most vintages from European vinifera can be purchased for between $12 and $20.

Relaxed and affordable does not mean cheap. For many decades, people assumed that only lower-grade wines could be produced in this snowy locale. Then scientists discovered that the extremely deep Finger Lakes create microclimates along their shores that make the growing of more delicate grapes possible. In 1976 the New York State government finally cleared away regulatory hurdles that had obstructed artisan vintners, and great winemakers began to immigrate to the area from around the world. Some dogged experimentation led to grafting of the best European vines onto cold- and disease-resistant American rootstock. Suddenly Finger Lakes vintages began to win blind taste tests even in places like France.

The meteoric rise of Finger Lakes wine is still in its early stages. But already the number of local wineries has jumped from a couple dozen to more than 130 (and counting), with large commensurate investments in vinifera grape plantings and all the accoutrements of great winemaking. And in the past few years Finger Lakes estates have won Wine Spectator scores in the 90s, and many other high honors—particularly for Rieslings, the region's signature wine.

* * *

The very same approaches that succeeded for grape growing and winemaking—unpretentious but highly innovative, open to new techniques, and intensely focused on quality—have been echoed in building up an exciting food scene in the Finger Lakes. And just as with wine, the landscape and soil were the first crucial assets.

Finger Lakes Food Joins Wine as Attraction for Visitors.

—Rochester Democrat & Chronicle

"The natural affinity between vineyard and farm," notes pioneering food writer Michael Turback, is that they are both wholly dependent upon their physical location. "What the French call *terroir* . . . refers to the geology and microclimate of a particular place, how the soil and the lakes are unmistakably expressed in the harvest, and how the disparate components of locale account for the uniqueness of our food and wine." The luscious fruits, vegetables, and other crops of the Finger Lakes reflect the area's rich natural inheritance.

Along with nature's blessing, the other irreplaceable component of great food is creative and industrious people. Here, too, the Finger Lakes are special. In his book *Summer in a Glass: The Coming of Age of Winemaking in the Finger Lakes,* reporter Evan Dawson documents the remarkable in-flow of talent which has brought clever growers, vintners, and managers to the area—and then united competitors in unusual cooperative ventures that have allowed the local wine industry to advance much more rapidly than in places where there is less mutual support.

The exact same phenomenon can be seen in the Finger Lakes food business. There is friendly exchange of information on the best suppliers; energetic collaboration among chefs and restaurants in establishing culinary tours, festivals, and classes; and frequent sharing of customers. Standards are high, yet there is an emphasis on learning and progressing together, and making sure that all diners have exciting and fun experiences. One result: New York State is now the number three destination in the nation for culinary tourists.

"I've worked in some of the best food and wine regions anywhere, and I've never seen anything like what's happening in this area," says executive chef Sean Agate of Our Heritage Café in Waterloo, New York. "This area is very agriculturally oriented—rustic, humble, friendly. There's almost no snobbery. Yet the people and institutions are smart and classy. And customers come here from all over the country and the world.

"Amazingly, there's none of the cutthroat attitude I ran into in the food business in other places," Agate continues, "where the goal is generally to put the neighboring restaurant out of business. Here people are much more interested in pulling each other up. There's a sense that we all win together."

One other ace card behind Upstate New York's culinary success is superb expert assistance. The most important institution has been Cornell University—an unusual place, which combines an Ivy League college, a powerful state agricultural school, some of the leading biological and botanical research centers in the country, the best hotel and hospitality school in the United States, the top veterinary school in America, and a long-standing emphasis on offering practical aid to farmers and food processors.

Cornell specialists have had a leading role in many food and agriculture breakthroughs: creation of popular new apple varieties, hybrid grape breeding, innovations in animal husbandry, important research on dairy products, a viticulture and enology program, hydroponic testing, running food labs, developing new cooking and processing technologies, consulting on ecological issues, and seeding its graduates throughout the region—where many of them have founded farms, vineyards, food-manufacturing companies, and restaurants. Other local educational institutions such as the Rochester Institute of Technology and Hobart and William Smith Colleges have also boosted the quality of local food production.

In addition, the village of Geneva in the heart of the Finger Lakes is home to two world-famous agricultural research stations devoted to improving U.S. fruits, vegetables, grains, meats, and other edibles. The U.S. Department of Agriculture Genetics Unit is responsible, among other things, for long-term preservation of the

seeds of tens of thousands of crops, as a protection against biological catastrophe.

Nearby, the New York State Agricultural Experiment Station is charged with advancing food production and farming practice in New York. It's easy to forget that New York is a largely rural state with more than 36,000 farms; seven million acres of land producing vegetables, fruits, dairy products, and meats; and total agricultural sales approaching $5 billion per year. With an annual budget over $25 million, 253 staff, 50 professors, up to 90 graduate students, and more than 50 miscellaneous scientists, the Experiment Station has helped make New York State the number five vegetable producer in the United States, despite its cold climate. With most production centered around the Finger Lakes region, New York ranks in the top five nationally in producing cabbage, sweet corn, onions, snap beans, cucumbers, squash, cauliflower, peas, pumpkins, maple syrup, apples, grapes, tart cherries, pears, and strawberries.

The ultimate sources of farm and culinary excellence in the Finger Lakes are lots of wise and progressive business people. We profile many producers in the pages that follow—from little nut-butter maker Once Again, to fruit-juice pioneers Red

Jacket Orchards, to Wegmans (which is not only a powerful leader among Finger Lakes food companies but actually America's top-rated grocer).

In recent years, the big pushes in cooking, eating, and food production have been to help Americans eat more wholesomely and help farmers use their land more gently. This cookbook shares those aspirations. You will find a good deal of information on healthful foods, and a particular emphasis on vegetables and fruits, especially locally grown crops.

As with many subjects, it's easy to hype or exaggerate natural-food claims.

Remember that nearly all nutrients are "chemicals," and that there are many, many completely naturally occurring compounds (like aflatoxins, molds, and pathogens) that are dangerous. The unevadable truth is that while this book was being written in 2011, more people were killed by bean sprouts from an organic farm in Germany (42 deaths after an *E. coli* outbreak) than by any man-made food additives or fertilizers.

It also must be acknowledged that free-ranging animals are at greater risk of some infections, since they live outdoors and are not administered antimicrobials.

Likewise, field crops grown with manures, a "natural" alternative to chemical fertilizer, can present their own health risks. It is for reasons like these that American and Canadian studies have found "natural" and "organic" foods around eight times more likely to be recalled than conventionally produced products.

There's another reason not to become zealous or unbending about "natural" production methods. Strict demands for organic production can dramatically increase the cost of vegetables, fruits, and grains, and those higher prices reduce consumption by everyday consumers. Turning "natural" production into a kind of substitute

Introduction

religion can thus actually be counterproductive, health-wise.

None of this means we should avoid organic food. To the contrary, many consumers are attracted to the organic ideal, and anything that encourages people to eat more fresh food is a good thing. It's simply important to avoid manias and take a moderate, balanced approach to eating. There are up sides and down sides to most of our choices in life, including something like organic food production.

Our view, directly reflected in the pages of this cookbook, is that the single best thing most Americans could do to improve their diet is to consume more fresh produce (vegetables and fruits in particular). That's why we are so supportive of farmer's markets and local sources of food. There is nothing fresher than the farm down the road.

And that's why we're encouraging you to eat less pre-prepared and processed food and to do more cooking for yourself!

Ultimately, we think food should be a source of satisfaction and pleasure, not stress or guilt. Eating is perfectly natural and necessary. From birth to adulthood we must ingest enough to power our daily actions and thoughts, and to increase our bulk roughly 25-fold. We are wise to enjoy that wholesome process.

And of course eating serves many wonderful social purposes. A fine meal is a higher thing than mere eating. Its goal, notes philosopher Leon Kass in his book *The Hungry Soul,* is "tasteful appreciation"—something that can ennoble all of life.

The quality of a meal, moreover, often influences the quality of dinner-table conversation. "Good talk and good food go naturally together . . . We come to ideas in the same way as we come to flavors, spices, textures," argues Kass. "The high play of thought and ideas, built around a meal, is a human ballet."

It's highly desirable that we take pleasure in the processes of acquiring and cooking food, since the act of eating itself is an entirely destructive undertaking.

Even the finest creation from a kitchen lasts for only a brief time—just a few moments for a hot meal, perhaps a year for a jar of pickles or glass of homemade jam. Great food, like theater, is thus a highly transient art.

"We must not get carried away by gourmandism," urges bioethicist Kass, for "the pleasures of taste are radically ephemeral. The enjoyed savor disappears almost immediately. Destruction is here the inescapable price of delight."

So do grab the moment, give yourself and loved ones a burst of primal sensation, and come feast! We've got some wonderful ideas to share from a beautiful region. We want you to read and cook with us, and then consume something memorable and healthy.

You'll put down your fork feeling fresh and fortified.

Almost as if you'd taken a dip in a cool, clear Finger Lakes waterfall.

Breakfasts

Nature is not our mother.

It is our sister.

We have the same Father.

—journalist G. K. Chesterton

Ann's Granola

Granola has become a very hot food item in recent years, but this recipe has been in heavy rotation in our household for decades. We keep a batch on hand most of the time, and consume it steadily for breakfast and snacks—with cold milk, or spooned over plain yogurt and topped with a bit of honey.

As with many homemade foods, this far, far surpasses store-bought granola in taste and appeal. It is crunchier, less sweet, has more range of flavor (not just oats), and includes lots of nuts, seeds, and fruit to keep things interesting. We never get tired of it (and often double or triple the recipe to make a quantity that will last a while). If you want variety, you can alter the ratios of the different ingredients.

This granola can also be sprinkled as a topping on fruit, ice cream, or baked fruit crisps. We used it to top a rhubarb crisp in the accompanying photo. The granola is beautiful jarred and presented as a gift. And it's very healthy.

4 cups uncooked rolled oats
½ cup sesame seeds
¾ cup raw sunflower seeds
1 cup wheat germ
½ cup raw cashews, raw almonds, or raw peanuts
A few tablespoons of whole or ground flax seed
⅓ cup honey
⅓ cup oil
2 Tablespoons water
¾ cup raisins, craisins, or both

Preheat oven to 300 degrees.

In a very large bowl, mix together oats, sesame seeds, sunflower seeds, wheat germ, nuts, and flax seed. Mix honey, oil, and water in a separate bowl, and pour this mixture over the dry ingredients. Stir well until uniformly coated.

Spread granola on a large cookie sheet or jelly-roll pan, and bake for 30 to 40 minutes until nicely browned. Stir the granola often while baking.

Remove from oven and cool. Stir in the dried fruit only after the granola is fully cooled (else the heat will dry it out). Or to altogether avoid the fruit getting dry and hard, just sprinkle it on each bowlful as you consume the granola. Store in a tightly sealed container to keep fresh.

Makes 7 cups.

Pear Bread

This recipe is reminiscent of a banana bread or an apple bread, but the flavor is distinct and pleasing, and the texture is especially nice. The riper and more flavorful the pears, the better the loaf—so try to buy local fruit and wait for it to fully ripen before firing up your oven.

> 1 stick butter, softened
> 1 cup sugar
> 2 eggs
> 1 teaspoon vanilla
> 2 cups flour
> ½ teaspoon baking soda
> 1 teaspoon baking powder
> ½ teaspoon nutmeg
> ¼ cup buttermilk or yogurt
> 1 cup ripe pears, peeled and chopped

Preheat oven to 350 degrees, and butter and flour a loaf pan.

With an electric beater, beat together the butter, sugar, eggs, and vanilla until creamy. In a separate bowl, blend together the flour, baking soda, baking powder, and nutmeg. Stir these dry ingredients into the butter mixture, then stir in buttermilk or yogurt, and finally the chopped pears.

Pour batter into pan and bake for 1 hour. Cool. Try serving with cold cream cheese. Makes 1 medium-size loaf.

Adapted from a recipe by Blackman Homestead Farm in Lockport, NY.

Capron Street Buttermilk Pancakes

If more people realized how easy it is to make pancakes from scratch—and, trust us, the light fluffiness and taste of these is like nothing out of a box—they'd realize the few extra minutes of labor are wholly worthwhile. This simple recipe was time-tested by Grandpa Taft, who churned out thousands of perfect little silver dollars for seven children on an old antique stove.

1¼ cups flour
1 teaspoon sugar
1 teaspoon baking powder
½ teaspoon baking soda
¼ teaspoon salt
1 egg, beaten
2 Tablespoons olive oil
1¼ cups buttermilk (plain yogurt makes a different, but interesting, pancake)

Slowly warm your griddle or frying pan. Don't use high heat while cooking—it's too easy to burn the outside of your cakes while the inside is still gooey.

Mix together the dry ingredients in a large bowl, then whisk in the wet ingredients.

Using a ladle or cup measure, spoon batter onto the medium-hot griddle or frying pan. We like to keep the cakes small, as they're easier to cook, and simpler to share among your waiting customers! Being careful not to burn the cakes, flip when bubbles begin to stay on the uncooked side. Serve with real maple syrup!

We love to add a dose of blueberries, chopped apple bits, or raspberries to the batter, or sometimes chopped pecans or walnuts.

Serves 4.

Orange Apricot Muffins

As long as you do your best not to overmix these, they will turn out to be the most deliciously creamy muffins you've ever had. They have a fruity surprise in the middle—the apricot preserves, which are also the secret to keeping the muffins so moist. These are best warm, but also good at room temperature. Treat them as an English-style afternoon treat, served with milky hot tea on some day when you're getting English-style weather outside.

1¾ cups flour
3 teaspoons baking powder
½ teaspoon baking soda
2 Tablespoons white sugar
2 Tablespoons brown sugar (light or dark)
½ teaspoon salt
1 egg
1 cup milk
½ stick butter, melted and cooled
1 Tablespoon grated orange zest
Apricot preserves

Preheat oven to 400 degrees.

In a large bowl, mix together the flour, baking powder, baking soda, sugars, and salt.

In a separate bowl, beat the egg lightly and then beat in the milk. Mix in the butter and orange zest.

Make a well in the dry ingredients and add the liquid all at once. With a wooden spoon, stir swiftly until just combined (10 to 15 strokes). Do not overmix, or the muffins will be tough. Spoon batter into 12 small or 6 large well-greased muffin wells, until the cups are about half full. Add a spoonful of apricot preserves on top, then cover with the remaining batter, until each well is about ¾ full.

Bake for 18 to 20 minutes, or until muffins are golden brown. Serve warm with butter.

Makes 12 small or 6 large muffins.

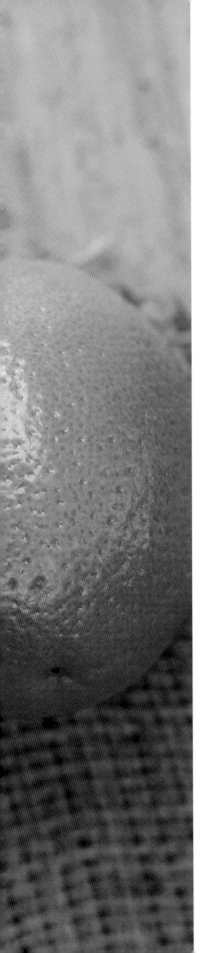

Kathy's Bran Muffins

Many bran muffins turn out dry and flavorless, yet are eaten because of their healthfulness. These are both nutritious and wondrously sticky, with lots of raisins. Eat them hot out of the oven with a pat of salted butter. Or toast them later.

2 cups raisins
1 large box of bran flakes cereal
1½ cups sugar
2½ cups white flour
2½ cups whole-wheat flour
4 teaspoons baking soda
2 teaspoons salt
4 eggs, beaten
1 quart buttermilk
1 cup vegetable oil

In a large mixing bowl, thoroughly combine raisins, cereal, sugar, flours, baking soda, and salt. In a separate bowl, whisk together eggs, buttermilk, and oil. Add the wet ingredients to the dry and stir no more than 15 times, or the muffins will be tough.

Let the batter sit on the counter for 45 minutes to allow the cereal to soften. Then fill greased muffin tins less than half full with batter. (If you own them, we much prefer large muffin tins over cup-cake size versions, as the larger muffins come out moister.)

Bake at 375 degrees for about 20 minutes. (Don't overcook or they will be dry.)

This makes a very large batch, but in a tightly sealed container the batter will keep in your refrigerator for a few weeks—ready to be spooned into muffin pans and popped into the oven morning after morning. Freshly baked muffins for breakfast don't have to be a fantasy!

Makes approximately 12–16 large muffins.

Flour as the Next Local Food

Fruits and vegetables were the first, comparatively simple, step in the revival of locally grown food. In many areas of the United States, local produce never disappeared. So when consumer interest rebounded, vegetables and fruits grown nearby readily returned to prominence in farmer's markets, grocery stores, and restaurants.

Locally produced meats and dairy products have been slower to appear. Even in many areas where there is clear consumer demand, it has taken a while to reestablish the butchering operations, yogurt- and cheese-making facilities, and other infrastructure needed to support regional production of meat and artisan dairy products. (Excessive government regulation has interfered with grassroots production of these local foods.)

Harder yet to restore is local grain milling. Grain is a huge part of modern diets, yet generations ago most U.S. production became centralized in the Great Plains. Specialized farm machinery, drying facilities, grain elevators, and grinding mills disappeared in many other parts of the country. Rochester, New York, was the greatest flour manufacturing center in the world shortly after the opening of the Erie Canal, shipping the production of 20 grist mills to New York City, England, and other parts of Europe. Today, there is nary a flour mill in Rochester. In most parts of the United States, in fact, local flour is extinct.

In Upstate New York, though, a local-flour revival is well under way. In Watertown there is an impressive new granite-stone grinding mill, called North Country Farms, that ships flours of exquisite flavor and texture across the state and into New York City and New England. North Country Farms sprang up so that the wheat grown along Lake Ontario didn't have to be expensively trucked out of state. When local farmer Ron Robbins and his wife decided to start a mill, they picked as manager a hometown man who had impressed them with his work ethic while playing basketball with their son.

Thanks to their entrepreneurial savvy, the white and whole-wheat flours of North Country Farms were, just three years later, available in hundreds of stores across

the state and are used by superb central New York bakeries like Old Heidelberg. North Country Farms also provides grain for the wheat beers made by local craft brewers. And it does this without the exorbitant prices sometimes associated with local production—actually charging a few cents less than mass-producers

Another brand-new startup, Farmer Ground Flour, produces stone-ground wheat flours (earthy whole-wheat for bread, whole-wheat pastry flour, and half-white) plus cornmeal, polenta, buckwheat, rye, and spelt flours. Farmer Ground Flour is located in Trumansburg, New York—in the heart of the Finger Lakes—and is a joint venture of a miller and two grain farmers.

A family operation that never stopped producing flours in Upstate New York is New Hope Mills—located in the Finger Lakes since 1823. One of their partners is Log City Milling, an operation in King Ferry, New York, that makes superb pastry flour.

Fresh artisan flours and baking mixes from these firms are available for purchase outside the area (see Resources section). Or search your own region for mills operating on this final frontier of the local-food revival.

You are likely to taste a difference. Many people don't realize that there are hundreds of variations of wheat, each with its own culinary qualities. For instance, the rich limestone-based soils of northern New York, combined with long, cold winters and dry summers with cool nights, produce hard red winter wheat that is perfect for bread making. The folks at Farmer Ground are experimenting with heirloom wheats, unusual corns, and innovative milling techniques.

The cooler stone-grinding process and lack of chemical bleaching give these flours a pleasant pinkish tinge and higher nutritional value. They have good protein, fiber, and gluten levels, and absorb more water during baking, giving products baked with them an exceptional "oven spring" and finished texture.

"When you open up a 50-pound bag, you get a whiff of springtime even in January," says Upstate New York craft baker and chef Doug Rountree.

Spiritual Reform
on Chautauqua Lake

The Chautauqua Institution is a quintessentially American institution where citizens have been trooping for nearly 140 summers to improve their minds, refine their souls, strengthen their bodies, and fire their spirits. Founded in 1874 by a Methodist minister and his friend (an inventor who became the father-in-law of Thomas Edison), Chautauqua is a place where generations of middle-Americans have refreshed, and sometimes even re-invented, themselves.

The first purpose of the institution was to educate and train Sunday School teachers from around the nation, so they could more effectively instruct and minister to their charges back home. The original assemblies were in tents pitched thickly along Chautauqua Lake in western New York. Over time, the grounds grew into a seasonal village of beautiful little cottages, outdoor lecture spaces, numerous chapels, several theaters, and recreation areas. The grounds are now listed as a National Historic Landmark.

Americans continue to flock to Chautauqua for religious inspiration, opportunities to improve their minds, and chances to develop their creative talents. All day long, there are lectures, Bible studies, art classes, concerts, dance performances, sports activities, sing-alongs, and study groups of all sorts. Every evening there is lively conversation around dinner tables and on packed front porches.

The Chautauqua Literary and Scientific Circle—which was founded to promote independent learning, particularly among those unable to attend formal schools—is the oldest book club in the United States. Much of the instruction at Chautauqua is self-guided, and the primary purpose behind spending a week or a summer at Chautauqua is to improve oneself.

This earnest do-it-yourself learning caused Teddy Roosevelt to describe the Chautauqua gatherings as "the most American thing in America." By the turn of the 20th century, this Upstate New York phenomenon had became so popular and influential it spawned several hundred other "Chautauquas" in locales across the country. The word thus entered the American lexicon to describe any assembly where Americans come together with the goal of self betterment.

Chautauqua Graham Bread

Here is a sweet brown bread that is just delightful: soft, flaky, very moist, with lots of whole-wheat and raisin flavor. If you prefer, you can bake it in muffin tins instead of as a loaf.

This is a century-old recipe from an iconic American cultural center, the Chautauqua retreat in Upstate New York (see facing page), based on the nutritional principles of an early American advocate of dietary reform (the zealous Sylvester Graham, who was an exponent of whole grains, among other causes).

Our original recipe from our Great-Grandmother Wilcox calls for "graham flour"— which is what the product milled from the whole kernel of wheat, including the bran and germ, was known as back when it was a nutritional innovation. Before you go tearing around looking for something ground from "graham" plants, rest assured that any whole-wheat flour from your local grocery will do the trick.

½ cup butter

1 cup brown sugar

2 eggs

2 cups buttermilk

1 cup raisins

2 teaspoons baking soda

2 teaspoons baking powder

1 teaspoon salt

2 cups whole-wheat flour

1 cup white flour

Preheat oven to 400 degrees.

Cream the butter and brown sugar together. Stir in the eggs, buttermilk, and raisins.

Mix the dry ingredients together in a small bowl. Then combine with the wet ingredients. Bake in greased bread-loaf pan for 45 minutes, or in greased muffin tins for 20 minutes.

Makes 1 medium-size loaf or 6 large muffins.

Sunday Morning Coffee Cake

This is a light coffee cake that's perfect for a weekend breakfast. It rarely lasts beyond the morning in our house. If you eat it a few minutes out of the oven, it will melt on your tongue. The butter drizzled on top causes the cinnamon sugar to sink down, streaking the golden cake with ribbons of sweetness.

¾ cup sugar
¼ teaspoon salt
1⅔ cups flour
3 teaspoons baking powder
1 cup milk
1 teaspoon vanilla
1 Tablespoon butter, melted
1 egg
1 teaspoon cinnamon
¼ cup sugar
¼ cup butter, melted

Grease a 9" x 13" pan and preheat oven to 350 degrees.

In a medium bowl, mix together the sugar, salt, flour, and baking powder. In a separate bowl, whisk up the wet ingredients. Then stir the wet ingredients into the dry, without overmixing.

Pour the batter into the prepared pan. In a small dish, mix together the cinnamon and sugar, then sprinkle over the batter. Finally, drizzle the melted butter over that.

Bake for 20 to 30 minutes.

Serves 8.

Grandma Z's Date Nut Bread

This is a marvelously sticky sweet bread, spiked with nuts, that anyone who likes dates will adore. Each rich bite is almost like chewing on a date. This has been eagerly gobbled up by at least four generations of our clan and will be baked in our family for many decades to come.

A note regarding the dates: there are many kinds of pitted dates available in stores, but we recommend, if possible, that you track down "block dates," sometimes also called "baking dates" (which tend to show up in stores particularly in the holiday season).

With block dates, the pitted fruit has been compressed into a dark square wrapped in plastic. We're not sure why, but much experimentation has taught us that the variety of dates used in those blocks makes for a much stickier, darker, and more delicious bread than is possible using the loose brown dates sold in containers or bags.

1¾ cups boiling water
2 cups chopped dates
1 Tablespoon butter, melted
2 cups sugar
1 egg, beaten
1 teaspoon vanilla
1 teaspoon salt
1½ teaspoons baking soda
2¾ cups flour
1 cup chopped walnuts

Preheat oven to 350 degrees. Grease two medium-size loaf pans and set aside. Pour the boiling water over the dates and let stand.

In a medium bowl, pour the melted butter over the sugar, mix, then add the egg and vanilla.

Stir the salt, baking soda, and flour into the sugar mixture, alternating with splashes of liquid from the date/water mixture. Beat the batter well.

Then stir in the nuts and the dates, along with any remaining water.

Pour the batter into the two pans and bake for 45 to 55 minutes, removing from oven as soon as a fork or toothpick comes out of the center clean.

Makes 2 loaves.

Bismarcks

In all likelihood, you've never heard of bismarcks. We rarely meet anyone who even has a clue as to what they are. We first discovered them in the fine *Silver Palate Cookbook,* from which we've adapted this recipe to our own taste. They are a delicious breakfast treat reminiscent of Yorkshire pudding. Compared with other sweet breakfasts like waffles or pancakes, bismarcks have a much lighter texture, but be sure to follow the directions exactly so they puff up as intended. They are a great foil for warm fresh fruit and real maple syrup—don't bother making them unless you have both of these crucial accompaniments.

4 Tablespoons butter
½ cup milk
½ cup all-purpose flour
2 eggs

Put butter in a heavy frying pan, or a shallow casserole dish, in 475-degree oven.

Mix milk, flour, and eggs lightly to make a batter. When the butter is completely melted and quite hot, quickly pour batter into pan and bake for 12 minutes. The bismarcks will puff up and then collapse, and end up as a thin, chewy crust that is golden brown and crunchy on the outside.

Remove from oven and cut into pieces. Spoon warmed fresh fruit onto each serving—our favorites are peaches, blueberries, or raspberries—and drown with heated maple syrup.

Serves 6.

*Adapted recipe from **Silver Palate Cookbook,** by Julee Rosso and Sheila Lukins.*

Vintage Maple Syrup

Of the myriad foods that man has figured out how to pluck from nature, maple syrup has always struck us as one of the most magical. In northern states with dense hardwood maple forests and muffling snows that shut down the metabolism of even the mightiest trees, there is an exceptionally brief window during the late-winter melt when a skilled maple-sugar maker can capture and refine one of biology's richest and most exotic foods: tree sap.

It's not simple. A maple tree must be at least 40 years old before it can be tapped; many of the specimens in a prime sugar bush are more than a century old. The weather must be just right—warm days and cold nights, else the sap will stop flowing or get milky and sour. Over the full 4 to 6 week season, a typical tree may yield enough sap for a quart to a gallon of finished syrup. Thus, substantial producers must tap hundreds of trees.

The sap must be hauled through snowy woods to a central location. And then the boiling commences. It takes about 43 gallons of sap (which ranges from 1–4 percent sugar) to yield a gallon of maple syrup (67 percent sugar, plus a nice concentration of minerals). The excess water is driven off via a wood fire under the syrup pan (which can add its own slightly smoky timbre to the syrup).

Authentic maple-syrup making is an important rural cottage industry in (by order of production) Vermont, New York, Maine, Wisconsin, Pennsylvania, Ohio, Michigan, and New Hampshire. One worrisome new threat to this all-American food is the Asian Longhorned Beetle, a destructive pest which snuck into the United States on cargo ships, has no natural predators in this country, and is particularly deadly to maple trees.

Every maple syrup, like every wine vintage, has its own flavor, depending on the soil, weather, and maker. We prefer medium or light ambers, which have a milder flavor than the dark grades. Buy from different producers and find your own favorites!

There are few greater pleasures for the discerning mouth than good pancakes or waffles drizzled in real maple syrup. Yet maple flavoring need not end at breakfast. This book includes several non-breakfast recipes; look for them in the index.

The Buckwheat Stops Here

Penn Yan is a handsome little Finger Lakes town that reigns as the buckwheat capital of America. Thanks to leaky farm trucks hauling in buckwheat seeds to be processed at the Birkett Mills right on Main Street (in continuous operation since 1797), the leafy green plant topped by sprays of white flowers now grows wild in ditches and pastures all across the area. One nice fringe benefit of the local buckwheat specialty: it is a superb source of nectar for honeybees, causing nearby hives to fill with a strong, dark sweetness.

Unrelated to wheat, and not even a grain or cereal, nutritious buckwheat was one of the earliest plants brought to the Americas by European settlers. Its short ten-week growing season, fondness for infertile soil, and preference for cool temperatures made it valuable to northern pioneers living on land newly scratched out of primeval forest.

Buckwheat pancakes were a staple in pioneer America. Later, immigrants from Poland and Russia cooked buckwheat groats almost like rice for their daily starch and protein. Buckwheat isn't all earthiness though—it's also the secret to fancy-pants French crepes. If you can't find buckwheat in your area, our Resources section will tell you how to get Finger Lakes products shipped to your door. (By the way, because buckwheat is entirely gluten free, it's prized by people with wheat allergies.)

Buckwheat Crepes

These authentic Breton-style crepes are delicate and yummy, and very easy to make. They can take on any personality, from savory to sweet, depending on what you fill them with.

1¼ cups buckwheat flour
¼ teaspoon salt
3 eggs
½ stick butter, melted
1 cup milk
1 cup water

Combine flour and salt in a large bowl. Whisk in eggs, melted butter, milk, and water. Batter will be very runny, much more so than pancake batter.

Heat an 8- or 10-inch nonstick skillet to medium-high. Apply a light coating of butter, and ladle or pour about a quarter cup of batter into hot pan. Pour in an expanding circular pattern, then tilt pan to spread batter even more, so crepe is as thin as possible. Don't worry, once browned they don't tear easily. If pan is too hot or too cool and batter doesn't start cooking immediately without burning, adjust heat accordingly.

After about a minute, use a non-stick spatula to loosen all around the rim of the crepe, then flip, using spatula and/or fingers. It may take one or two sacrificial crepes, but you'll get a rhythm. As the second side lightly browns (usually about another minute), slide crepe onto a plate.

Either serve immediately, rolled up around your favorite filling, or stack them, with waxed paper or plastic wrap between each, for heating and serving later.

Crepes can be filled with fresh fruits or preserves, cheese and ham, eggs and spinach, Nutella, honey and yogurt, ice cream, whatever you like. The Blackman fruit butters and Once Again nut butters (see following pages) make superb crepe fillings; you might want to top with a dollop of whipped cream.

Crepes that have cooled, or been frozen for later use, can be heated on a cookie sheet in a 375-degree oven, either before or after rolling them around their filling.

Makes about 12 crepes.

Fruit & Nut Butters

Pristine local fruit often makes its way into preserves. Among many delicious examples from the Finger Lakes region, the fruit butters of the Blackman Homestead Farm have particular appeal. The sixth generation of the Blackman family creates these flavored fruit butters at their own orchards in the rich Niagara Escarpment. The fruit butters make superb crepe fillings and can also be used as spreads, mixed with yogurts, in any cooking where a concentrated fruit essence is desired, or in specialized uses listed below. Ordering information is provided in our Resources section; or you may be able to obtain similar products in your home region.

Apple Walnut Butter or Apple Cinnamon Butter (mild and tasty)
Fill the cavity of an acorn squash and bake
Spread over pork chops while grilling
Offer as a condiment with pork tenderloin
Serve with cheddar or Gouda cheese on crackers

Cherry Almond Butter (strong almond and cherry bite)
Use as a filling in cookies or between cake layers
Slather over a block of cream cheese and serve with crackers
Use as a topping on desserts

Pumpkin Maple Butter (brisk flavor of pumpkin spices)
Use as a cake filling or a topping on cheesecake
Substitute for mayonnaise on ham or turkey sandwiches
Spread on ham at the end of baking
Use on pancakes instead of butter, then drizzle with maple syrup

Pear and Port Butter or Pear Vanilla Butter (rich and sweet)
Serve with blue cheese or hard Parmesan on crackers or thin bread slices

Use as a condiment with lamb
Spread over peanut butter on toast or English muffins

Excellent nut and seed butters are also created in the Finger Lakes region by an intriguing employee-owned, award-winning company known as Once Again. A pioneer in the natural-food industry, the business is based in the historic rural New York town of Nunda (pronounced "none day"), population 3,000.

Once Again makes several different kinds and flavors of almond butter, cashew butter, and peanut butter. There are creamy and crunchy versions of each, even a formulation that adds flax seed oil to create food high in healthy omega-3. The company also manufactures tahini (sesame seed butter) and sunflower seed butter.

For more examples of how to use these interesting products, see Almond-Butter Brownies, p. 171; Almond/Cashew Chicken Salad p. 103; Peanut Butter Mousse, p. 173; Tahini-Yogurt Lemon Dressing & Dipping Sauce, p. 125.

Once Again is a producer, as well, of honey from hives in Upstate New York and New England. Through their partnerships with nut farmers in the tropics, they also started selling tropical honeys collected by rural beekeepers in Central and South America. They even offer Killer-Bee Honey—one flavor from Brazil, another from Nicaragua.

Killer bees were originally brought from Africa to the Americas in the hope of improving honey production. They proved to be good pollinators, but less productive makers of honey than existing bees. Nonetheless, they are here to stay, and their honey has its own particular flavor profile, not to mention shock value on the table.

Collecting honey from killer bees can be tricky. The Once Again collectors not only wear traditional bee-keeper suits but also always bring a partner with them. The partner waits in a running pickup truck, so that if the bees start to swarm, the bee keeper can escape more quickly.

Once Again nut and seed butters and honeys are distributed nationally—consult the Resources section for details on finding them.

Buckwheat Pancakes

1 cup buckwheat flour
½ teaspoon salt
1 teaspoon baking soda
1 cup water or milk
1 egg
2 teaspoons maple syrup, honey, molasses, or sugar
¼ teaspoon vanilla (optional)

Beat all ingredients together. Adjust liquid or flour to make batter flow to desired thickness. Cook on a greased griddle or frying pan.

For variations, add chopped apples or blueberries, diced ham, or ½ teaspoon of pumpkin-pie spice.

Serves 4.

Breakfasts

Soups
& Appetizers

Easy to please, hard to satisfy.

—writer George MacDonald's

characterization of God

Cider-Vinegar Chili

Our entire extended family adores this chili. Its mix of sweetness and vinegar tartness makes it very different from southwestern-style chilis. As the last step in making the dish, we balance the sweet/sour level to taste and often find ourselves adding more than the amount of vinegar the recipe calls for—feel free to do the same. The flavor of this chili improves over time, so if possible prepare it a day before serving, or at least let it cool and reheat once thoroughly to encourage the necessary melding of flavors.

> 4 medium onions, chopped
> 1½ pounds ground beef
> 2 small cans red kidney beans, rinsed
> 2 cans white or black beans, rinsed
> 2 large (30 ounce) cans diced tomatoes
>   or tomato juice
> 3 Tablespoons chili powder
> 3 Tablespoons apple-cider vinegar
> ¼ cup sugar
> 1 cup water
> 1 teaspoon salt
> Freshly ground black pepper

In a large pot, sauté the onions and ground beef until cooked. If your beef is fatty, you might want to pour or spoon off excess oil.

Then add all the other ingredients, and let simmer for 30 minutes or longer. Taste and adjust vinegar and seasonings.

If you are serving it the same day, let chili sit on the stovetop off the heat until ready to warm and dish up. Or refrigerate until ready to heat and serve.

Makes 8–10 servings.

Salmon & Dill Chowder

Suzanne Stack, a James Beard Award–nominated chef, reports that her mother served soup before almost every meal. As a result, Suzanne adores soups of all kinds, including this marvelous, uncomplicated chowder. When she makes it, three ingredients come from her garden, and all of the others from farms within a few miles of her hilltop restaurant, which is located in the epicenter of the Finger Lakes food and wine belt.

4 bacon slices
1 medium onion, diced
3 stalks celery, diced
1 leek, diced
1 large carrot, diced
3 medium potatoes, cut
    into 1-inch cubes
1 quart chicken stock
1 pound salmon filet,
    cut into 1-inch cubes
1 cup heavy cream
1 cup milk
2 Tablespoons chopped
    fresh dill
3 Tablespoons butter
Dill fronds
Diced tomato

Cook and drain the bacon, then sauté the onion, celery, leek, and carrot in some bacon fat until slightly softened. Place sautéed vegetables in a pot with the potatoes and stock, and simmer for 15 minutes. Then add salmon. As soon as potatoes are cooked through, add the cream, milk, dill, and butter, and bring to serving temperature. Garnish each bowlful with bacon pieces, dill fronds, and diced tomato.

Makes 6 servings.

Adapted from a recipe by Suzanne Fine Regional Cuisine in Lodi, NY.

Savory Lentil, Garlic & Cumin Soup

Though quite simple to make, this is highly flavorful and the texture is a delight. Unlike pea soup, lentils stay within their capsules and do not turn into mush, so they are fun on the tongue. And unlike pea soup this is spicy, not sweet.

2 quarts chicken stock
2 cups dried lentils
1 onion, chopped
1 tomato, chopped
2 teaspoons diced garlic
4 Tablespoons butter
2 Tablespoons ground cumin
1 teaspoon salt
Freshly ground black pepper to taste

Bring chicken stock to a boil. Add all other ingredients. Reduce heat to low and simmer covered for 45 minutes.

Makes 8 servings.

Food—Iroquois Style

The Iroquois (or Haudenosaunee in their own language) were the most successful farmers of any northern American Indian group. In their fertile central New York homeland, they cleared and then tilled large fields, made maple syrup, grew pumpkins, and planted extensive fruit orchards. Their main field crops were the "three sisters" (corn, beans, and squash), which they planted together symbiotically.

Corn (which is native to the Americas and was unknown to Europeans) was the staple food of the Iroquois, but it sucks nitrogen out of the soil at a rate which soon depletes fertility. Beans, however, harbor fungi in their roots, which pull nitrogen out of the atmosphere and "fix" it in the soil, thus actually making the earth richer as they grow—a perfect match for the voracious feeding of corn. Cornstalks in the Iroquois fields also gave the bean vines something to climb, increasing their growth and output. Meanwhile, the squash plants, mingled within the same fields, created a dense mat of leaves, which suppressed weed growth and retained soil moisture.

This was intelligent agriculture.

Three-Sisters Soup

The Iroquois typically kept a pot of soup or mash containing corn, along with beans and squash, simmering over the fire all day long, dipping into it whenever they were hungry. During most of the year, when fresh corn was unavailable, they used dried corn, often processed with wood ashes to make white hominy. A favorite addition to the soup was the head of a bear.

Corn soup remains the most important Iroquois food today, and many versions are served by Mohawk, Oneida, Onondaga, Cayuga, and Seneca families living around the Finger Lakes. This is our own modernized version, and it's tasty.

8–10 ears sweet corn (about 6 cups of kernels—
    may substitute frozen corn if fresh is unavailable)
1 pound bacon
3 quarts chicken broth
2 cups water
1 cup uncooked rice, preferably wild
1 cup lima, kidney, or pinto beans (fresh, frozen, or canned)
1 cup cubed summer or zucchini squash
1 large onion, chopped
1 large green pepper, chopped
Large handful of dandelion or other clean wild greens
    (may substitute thinly sliced cabbage, kale, spinach,
    or other greens)
Salt and pepper to taste
Fresh basil leaves or other herbs to taste

Roast corn lightly on an outdoor grill. (You can boil ears instead if you lack a grill.) Once the ears have cooled, cut kernels off the cob.

Fry the bacon lightly (do not approach crispness), discard oil. Chop bacon into bite-sized pieces.

Pour chicken broth into large (8 quart) pot. Add all ingredients. Cook over low heat until rice is done.

If you're feeling adventurous, serve a small bowl of buttered popcorn as croutons.

Makes 5–6 quarts. (Freezes well for later use.)

Artisan Oils

One hundred fifty years ago, Hiram Hotchkiss of New York's Ontario County became the world leader in the production of high-quality oil from locally grown peppermint plants. Today, the Finger Lakes region continues to produce interesting edible oils.

The same cooperative of grape-farmers that we rely on for our Concord drinking juice (see Resources section) also produces a cold-pressed, unrefined cooking oil from the seeds of their grapes (the only Concord grape-seed oil made in the United States). It is light, mild, and olive oil-like, but with a hint of cinnamon flavor at the end. Unlike olive oils, it is a local product, not imported from overseas.

More exotic and strong flavored are the oils produced in Geneva, New York, from four winter squash varieties that are cold-weather staples on Finger Lakes dinner tables. A few years ago, two artisan bakers who had just moved to the Finger Lakes region from Boston were approached by a local farmer and asked if they could help him find a use for the seeds that were then a waste product of his butternut squash–growing operation. With the help of food scientists from Cornell University, they created an all-natural way to roast the seeds in small batches and then press a distinctive vegetable oil from them without added heat or chemicals.

Today, Stony Brook cooking oils are made from four varieties of local squash: butternut, buttercup, acorn, and delicata. Each has a different nutty flavor and deep color. Each is high in unsaturated fat and rich in vitamins A and E compared with other vegetable oils. We are still discovering uses for them: as a dressing for salads containing smoked or grilled meats, with sautéed vegetables, drizzled over pasta or potatoes, as dipping oil—a new finding every week!

These culinary oils—the only ones produced in the United States from by-product vegetable seeds—can be purchased in New York City and upstate, as well as in stores in New England, the mid-Atlantic, Michigan, California, and Utah. They are also available by mail. See Resources section.

Good News Soup

This is a delicious Italian-style vegetable soup, very fresh and nourishing. We adapted it out of a recipe from a dear woman who taught Sunday School to one of our sons in Ithaca.

¼ cup grape-seed or olive oil
¼ cup of each, chopped: celery, onions, carrots,
    and fennel (bulb and greens)
1 garlic clove, diced
6 cups chicken broth
¼ teaspoon dried thyme
1 Tablespoon chopped cilantro
2 cups peeled and cubed potatoes
1½ cups cannellini beans, drained and rinsed
3 cups diced fresh tomatoes (or canned)
1½ cups shredded Swiss chard or savoy cabbage
1 cup zucchini, cubed small
½ teaspoon salt
Freshly ground black pepper
Grated cheese

In a large soup kettle, combine oil, celery, onions, carrots, fennel, and garlic. Sauté vegetables 5 to 10 minutes over medium heat.

Then stir in broth, thyme, cilantro, potatoes, beans, tomatoes, and chard or cabbage. Heat to boiling, then reduce heat and simmer for 15 minutes.

Add zucchini; cover and cook for 5 more minutes. Adjust salt and pepper to taste.

Sprinkle with grated cheese (Asiago, Swiss, Romano, or other) and serve.

Makes 8 servings.

Mussels
in Coconut & Saffron Broth

One of the delights of mussels served in a scrumptious broth like this is the inevitable bread-dipping that is not only allowed but encouraged. This coconut and saffron broth, infused with the flavors of garlic, white wine, and of course the mussels, is too delicious to waste. So be sure to remember the bread!

If you've never cooked mussels, don't be intimidated. You'll know they're done when they open. The most important thing is to make sure they are well cleaned.

1 Tablespoon olive oil
1 Tablespoon chopped shallots
½ Tablespoon chopped garlic
Pinch of cracked red pepper
2 pounds fresh mussels
Pinch of saffron threads
½ cup vermouth (or any dry white wine)
1 cup coconut milk
Salt

¼ cup chopped chives
¼ cup chopped parsley
French bread

In a large pan, heat olive oil and then sauté the shallots, garlic, and red pepper until fragrant, about one minute. Add the mussels, saffron, white wine, and coconut milk. Season with salt. Cover the pan and steam the mussels until they open. (This will take just a few minutes.) Discard any that don't open.

Meanwhile, slice French bread and grill until crusty (or simply wrap a baguette in tin foil and put in a hot oven for a few minutes). Once mussels are cooked, sprinkle with chives and parsley. Serve with French bread.

Serves 4–6 as an appetizer.

Adapted from a recipe by Zabroso in Oneida, NY.

Duxelles

This is a handy mushroom preparation you can use to add flavor to other foods.

½ cup chopped shallots or onion
3 Tablespoons butter or olive oil
2 cups fresh mushrooms (shiitakes or oysters work well),
    chopped or food-processed as finely as is convenient
Dash of salt and pepper
You may add garlic, ginger, or thyme to taste, if desired

Sauté shallots or onion in butter or oil until transparent. Add mushrooms and cook until the liquid released by the mushrooms evaporates and the mixture becomes thick. Season with salt and pepper. Add other seasonings, if desired.

Use immediately, refrigerate for later, or freeze. Spoon into sauces, soups, eggs, stuffings; use as a side relish with meats or fish; or serve on toast as a light meal.

Makes 1 cup.

Mushroom Cauliflower Soup

An earlier version of this recipe came to us through an aunt who returned from a year of living in Norway with some exquisite knitting and this cold-weather comfort broth. It is a mild soup that celebrates subtle vegetable tastes by keeping the surrounding flavors very mellow. If you like mushrooms and the crumble-in-your-mouth texture that cauliflower acquires after it has been simmered, this will appeal.

1 head cauliflower, cut into
  chunks
1 cup of your favorite
  mushrooms, chopped
5 Tablespoons butter, divided
¼ cup flour
2 cups chicken broth
2 cups beef broth
Salt and ground pepper,
  to taste

Boil cauliflower in two cups of water until it begins to become tender, but don't overcook into mushiness. Separate cooked cauliflower from the liquid—and save the liquid.

While cauliflower is cooking, sauté mushrooms in half of the butter for about 10 minutes.

In a good-sized pot, melt the remaining butter, add the flour, and mix until smooth. Add the hot cauliflower broth and stir hard until lumps are gone. Add chicken and beef broths, salt and pepper, and bring to a boil. Add the cauliflower and mushrooms and simmer for 10 minutes. Break the cauliflower into small pieces if it isn't already.

Serves 4–6.

Mushrooms
Will Inherit the Earth

Mushrooms are not plants: they are the fruits of funguses. The parent mycelium live mostly underground, and they can be some of the largest and oldest living organisms on earth. One honey-mushroom colony in eastern Oregon is thought to be at least 2,400 years old and to extend under the soil for about three and one-half square miles.

Specialized cultivators increasingly grow fancy mushrooms for sale at farmer's markets. Generally this is done by inoculating hardwood logs with spores. Because mushrooms are quite perishable and don't ship well, this is mostly a local specialty in places like the Finger Lakes.

Mushrooms can be dried, however, and then kept for more than a year for use in cooking. Local dried mushrooms can be substituted for the fresh variety in many dishes. One Finger Lakes grower who ships a gourmet blend of dried chanterelle mushrooms is Blue Oyster Cultivation (see Resources section).

Creole Sausage
on Jack Cornbread

This is a fun, visually appealing, and rich finger food. If you prefer to make cornbread from a box, that'll work fine—just add the cheese and creamed corn to the mix. New Hope Mills sells both a nice corn meal if you're making your own bread, and a good mix if you want a shortcut (see Resources section).

Creole Mayonnaise

    ¼ cup mayonnaise

    2 Tablespoons chopped sun-dried tomatoes

    1 teaspoon creole seasoning

    1 teaspoon meat rub (any hot, smoky seasoning you like)

    Sprinkle of fresh chives and fresh parsley (save for garnish)

Mix ingredients, except chives and parsley, until well blended. Store in fridge until ready to use.

Jack Cornbread

1¼ cups flour

¾ cup corn meal

¼ cup sugar

4½ teaspoons baking powder

½ teaspoon salt

1 egg

1 cup milk

¼ cup olive oil

½ cup Monterey Jack cheese, shredded

1 can (about 9 ounces) creamed corn

Preheat oven to 425 degrees.

Grease a 9" x 12" baking pan. Mix the five dry ingredients.

In a separate bowl, mix the egg, milk, oil, cheese, and creamed corn. (Drain excess liquid off corn.)

Fold the dry and wet ingredients together until just combined. Do not overmix.

Pour into pan and bake until bread springs back when you touch its center (about 15 minutes). Cool for 15 minutes, remove from pan and slice into 1½-inch squares.

Sausage

½ pound hot Italian sausage

Remove meat from casing and make small patties the size of a quarter. Fry until cooked thoroughly.

To assemble a plate of the appetizers, place a dab of creole mayonnaise and a sprinkling of fresh chives on each cornbread square, then top with sausage.

Serves 8–10 as an appetizer.

Adapted from a recipe by The Belhurst in Geneva, NY.

Butternut Bisque with Apple Kasha

This sweet, creamy soup offers a rich palate, thanks to the density of spicing. The kasha garnish adds just the right nutty texture and apple overtone.

Kasha

1½ Tablespoons onion, minced

1 apple, diced

2 teaspoons Stony Brook squash-seed oil (see Artisan Oils on page 50)

½ cup buckwheat groats (kasha)

1¼ cup cider

½ teaspoon salt

¼ teaspoon ground nutmeg

Bisque

1 butternut squash, peeled, seeded, and cut into golf ball–size chunks

2 ripe tomatoes

2 cups cider

1 Tablespoon dried tarragon leaves

½ teaspoon ground coriander

¼ teaspoon ground ginger

1 teaspoon ground white pepper

¼ teaspoon ground allspice

1 teaspoon ground cinnamon

½ teaspoon salt

1 pint half and half

To make the bisque, place squash, tomatoes, cider, and seasonings in a stockpot and bring to a rolling boil. Once squash is fork tender, cool for a while, then purée in a blender or food processor. (You will probably need to do this in two batches.) Return the purée to the stockpot and add half and half. Bring to a slow simmer, stirring occasionally to prevent scorching. Soup will naturally thicken and become velvety after about 20 minutes. Season with additional salt to taste.

When you are ready to serve, heat the bisque. Reheat the kasha and fluff it with a fork. Ladle soup into bowls, then place a large spoonful of kasha in the center of the liquid.

Makes 6 servings.

Adapted from a recipe by The Restaurant at Knapp Vineyards in Romulus, NY.

Spinach & Brussels Sprouts Dip

How many party dishes feature these two healthy vegetables? You can experiment with different cheeses, and be creative about the foods you offer your guests to dip with.

½ pound spinach, steamed and then cooled
1 pound brussels sprouts, steamed and cooled,
    then sliced into shreds
1 cup shredded mozzarella cheese
½ cup grated Parmesan cheese
2 teaspoons garlic powder
½ teaspoon crushed red pepper
1 cup mayonnaise
Salt and pepper to taste

Mix all ingredients together, place in an oven-safe bowl or baking dish, and bake at 400 degrees for 5 to 8 minutes.

Serve with bread (toasted or not), tortilla chips, or crackers.

Serves a crowd, as an appetizer.

Adapted from a recipe by Sean Agate, chef at Our Heritage Cafe in Waterloo, NY.

Papas Bravas

This tapa is delicious, thanks to the aioli (a sort of creamy, garlicky, homemade mayonnaise). In some parts of the country the chipotles—smoked jalapeno peppers—may be a little difficult to find; check the Mexican section of your grocery store, or an ethnic or gourmet food store.

Roasted Garlic

10 whole cloves of garlic, peeled
1 cup of grape-seed or olive oil
5 large sprigs of fresh thyme
Pinch of salt

Roasted Potatoes

1 pound potatoes (Yukon Gold work well)
1 Tablespoon grape-seed or olive oil
Sprinkling of salt

Aioli

2 egg yolks
½ Tablespoon Dijon mustard
Juice of 1 lemon
Salt
Oil reserved from roasting of garlic
¼ can chipotle peppers in adobo, chopped
Roasted garlic cloves, mashed with a fork

Preheat oven to 400 degrees. Place the garlic cloves, oil, thyme, and salt in an oven-proof dish and cover with tin foil.

Next, cut the potatoes into wedges, coat them with oil and some salt, and arrange in one layer on a sheet pan.

Roast the potatoes and garlic, in their separate pans, in the same 400-degree oven. They should both be ready within about 30 minutes.

As soon as the garlic cloves are soft, remove pan from oven and let cool. Discard the thyme, and separate the cloves from the oil—saving both.

Soon after the garlic, the potatoes should be done—test for softness. Remove from oven.

While the roasting is taking place, start the aioli. Place the egg yolks, mustard, lemon juice, and a pinch of salt in a bowl. As soon as the garlic cloves are roasted and set aside, pour the garlicky oil into the aioli and slowly whisk until the ingredients are well emulsified. Add the chopped chipotle peppers. Then mash the roasted garlic and add that.

To serve, coat the potatoes with the roasted-garlic aioli. To serve this dish in a party setting, arrange the potato wedges on a platter, slather with the scrumptious sauce, and supply sturdy toothpicks for spearing.

Serves 4–6.

Adapted from a recipe by Zabroso in Oneida, NY.

Rare Food
in a "Burned-Over" Landmark

The Finger Lakes region has always had a deep idealistic streak. Reflecting the many utopian causes (religious, political, artistic, and educational) that flared through central and western New York across two centuries, historians refer to the area as the "burned-over district."

This was a hotbed for social movements such as abolitionism, temperance, and female suffrage. Seventh-day Adventism, Mormonism, Spiritualism, Millerism and several other religious innovations were born here. The Underground Railroad operated throughout the area, guiding escaped slaves over the border into Canada.

One of the oddest utopian experiments in America was based in Oneida, New York. At its peak, a couple hundred intelligent, unconventional questers practiced a bizarre mixture of "Bible communism," highly successful Yankee commerce, diligent self-improvement, creepy eugenics, and daffy "free love."

The Oneida Community had its own dairy and grew a wide variety of vegetables and fruits. During the 1870s, railway excursions brought hundreds of visitors to the Community grounds to see what manner of people lived there, and to eat the Community's famous group dinners—which were mostly vegetables, fruits, and breads.

The Oneidans were early advocates for the importance of fresh local ingredients in good cooking. In their book *Oneida Community Cooking,* published in 1873, they note that if their cooks "depended on a city market for provisions, their greatest skill would not avail to give the flavor which so much charms." The renown given to their food stemmed from their access to "genuine cream, sweet butter, new-laid eggs, berries fresh from the vines, fruit just picked, peas, beans, tomatoes and all other vegetables at their best. Freshness is the sauce and seasoning for everything."

The Oneidans built this impressive Mansion House, which served as the center of their activities. Listed as a National Historic Landmark, it now hosts a museum, a bed-and-breakfast, and handsome rental apartments. A very fine restaurant called Zabroso was also originally housed in the Mansion House and has now grown to a new location nearby. Chef Ruben Lopez (whose wife is a native of the area) was born in Spain and trained at the Culinary Institute of America in the Hudson Valley, and now adds a delightful Latin twist to the local food scene.

Herbed Potato Soup

The defining characteristic of this robust soup is the depth and dimension lent to it by the herbs. If herbs are not your cup of tea, you could certainly dial them down—although we highly recommend you don't.

2 Tablespoons butter
2 large onions, thinly sliced
1 leek, thinly sliced
1 celery stalk, thinly sliced
3 slices bacon, chopped
1 Tablespoon dried marjoram
   (or dried oregano)
1 Tablespoon dried thyme
¼ Tablespoon nutmeg
1 pound potatoes,
   peeled and thinly sliced
4 cups chicken broth
1 Tablespoon salt
¼ Tablespoon black pepper
2 Tablespoons chives,
   freshly snipped (for garnish)

Melt butter in a large pot over moderate heat. Add the onions, leek, celery, bacon, marjoram, thyme, and nutmeg, and sauté about two minutes. (You can substitute fresh herbs for dried in any recipe by multiplying the dried quantity by 2½.)

Reduce heat to low, cover and steam 15 minutes until onions are limp. Raise heat to moderate, add potatoes and broth, and bring to a simmer. Cover and simmer 40 minutes, until the potatoes are soft.

Remove pan from heat and cool, still covered, for 15 minutes. Then purée in a food processor or blender in batches. Return soup to pan, mix in salt and pepper, taste and adjust seasoning as needed. Heat soup, uncovered, to serving temperature, ladle into bowls, and garnish with chives.

Serves 4–6.

Adapted from a recipe by Castel Grisch in Watkins Glen, NY.

Dano's Liptauer

Liptauer is a zesty cheese spread that has origins in Slovakia, Hungary, Germany, Austria, and Italy. It is deliciously spiced, and the chopped radish lends a beautiful crunch. There are many ways to make it and many possible variations—Seneca Lake Chef Dano Hutnik (a 2012 nominee for the James Beard Award) lists his final three ingredients below as "optional." We highly recommend adding them all, however. You may serve liptauer as a spread on hearty bread or as a dip with vegetable slices.

½ stick butter at room temperature
1 cup feta cheese
1 cup cream cheese at room temperature
1 clove garlic, minced fine
1 small onion, minced fine
2 teaspoons caraway seed
3 Tablespoons sweet Hungarian paprika
Salt and pepper to taste
Chopped radish
Pinch of cayenne pepper
2 anchovy filets
1 Tablespoon capers

Cream butter and feta using an electric hand-mixer, then beat in the cream cheese. Fold in the rest of the ingredients by hand.

Serve on toasted pumpernickel bread with a garnish of fresh parsley, chopped radish, or cherry tomatoes.

Serves a crowd.

Adapted from a recipe by Dano's Heuriger on Seneca, just south of Lodi, NY.

Apricot Black Bean & Verjus Salsa

This is a yummy and pretty-on-the-plate starter. Apricot season is quite short—and some years it doesn't come at all—but if apricots are not available, peaches can be a substitute.

Verjus is a wonderful regional specialty, a pungent juice that comes from wine grapes that are picked and squeezed before they are ripe. See Resources section for a Finger Lakes supplier that will ship to your home. If you must substitute, use half lemon juice and half red wine vinegar as an alternative to verjus.

2 cups diced apricots
2 cups (1 can) black beans, drained
¼ cup chives, chopped
2 Tablespoons fresh cilantro, chopped
2 Tablespoons garlic, pressed
1 Tablespoon parsley, chopped
2 Tablespoons white wine
2 Tablespoons verjus
1½ teaspoons sugar
1½ Tablespoons olive oil
Juice of half a lemon
Salt and pepper to taste

In a large bowl, mix together apricots, beans, chives, cilantro, garlic, and parsley. In a separate small bowl, mix together wine, verjus, sugar, olive oil, and lemon juice until sugar is dissolved. Pour over apricot mixture and sprinkle with salt and pepper.

You may serve this salsa with tortilla chips, or on top of grilled chicken, pork, or fish.

Makes 4–5 cups of salsa.

Adapted from a recipe by Red Newt Bistro in Hector, NY.

Scallion & Goat Cheese Crostini

This scallion-and-cheese mix is presented as an appetizer on bread. If you prefer, you could serve it dolloped atop a steak or on pasta. The white-wine flavor is vivid.

Handful of scallions, ramps, or young onions
½ cup white wine
Olive oil
Salt and pepper to taste
2 bay leaves
1 orange, cut into thin slices
1 baguette
Garlic-and-herb goat cheese
Chives, chervil, tarragon, Italian parsley, or
   other flavorful herb chopped roughly

Chop the scallions and place in a baking pan. Pour the wine on top, drizzle with olive oil, and sprinkle generously with salt and pepper. Lay the bay leaves on top of the scallions, and the orange slices on top of that.

Cover with foil and bake for 30 to 40 minutes, until tender. Discard the orange slices and bay leaves.

To assemble the crostini, slice the baguette on the bias, and lay the slices on a cookie sheet. Drizzle them with olive oil and crumble the goat cheese on top. Either bake or broil until crisp.

Then pile the scallions onto the cheese, sprinkle with herbs, and serve.

Serves 8–10 as an appetizer.

Adapted from a recipe by Just a Taste in Ithaca, NY.

Blackened Blue Fondue

This is a perfect party dish—rich and decadent, and your guests will need just a taste to feel satisfied. Serving it with apple slices instead of bread is a refreshing alternative.

½ pound crabmeat
1 Tablespoon Cajun seasoning
1 Tablespoon grape-seed or
vegetable oil
1 cup Gewürztraminer
(or other white wine)
1 Tablespoon fresh lemon juice
½ pound Gruyère cheese,
shredded
½ pound blue cheese,
crumbled
2 Tablespoons cornstarch
1 garlic clove, minced
½ teaspoon dry mustard
Small pinch of nutmeg
1 Tablespoon sweet sherry
(optional)
16 tart apple slices
16 slices crusty baguette

Coat the crabmeat with Cajun seasoning. In a heavy frying pan, heat the oil until it is very hot. Add the crab (be careful of the crabmeat "popping" when you add it to the oil) and let the seasoning blacken slightly. Set aside.

In a new pan, bring the wine and lemon juice to a simmer over low to medium heat. Coat the cheeses with cornstarch, then slowly add them while stirring (do not heat too quickly or too high). Add the garlic, mustard, nutmeg, and sherry. Finally, add the seasoned crab.

Serve with apples and baguette slices for dipping.

Serves 8–10.

Adapted from a recipe by The Belhurst in Geneva, NY.

The Return of Local Cheese

Once upon a time, most villages in the Finger Lakes, and other dairying regions across the United States, had their very own "cheese factory"—usually a cooperative where local farmers brought milk to be cultured and aged into various cheese types. Then cheese production went national, and many people assumed the era of widespread local cheese making was over for good.

Not so. Founded only at the end of 2003, the New York State Farmstead & Artisan Cheese Makers Guild now counts 36 members, and growing. Many other makers operate outside the guild. Some other states have seen a similar rebirth of locally made cheese.

In the Finger Lakes region, a group of eleven farmstead cheese-making operations joined together in 2010 in a "cheese trail" designed to appeal to travelers touring the local wine trails. They offer cow-, goat-, and sheep-milk creations, in dozens of varieties and flavors.

As a food product, local cheeses are following a trajectory similar to American wines—showing rapid growth in quality and supply from many new small-scale producers. Most of these producers sell only in their immediate area, so search out your own local-farm-cheese favorites.

Main Dishes

Standards are always out of date;

that's why they are called standards!

—playwright Alan Bennett

Pork Tenderloin with Peach Salsa

This dish is spicy, yet scrumptiously balanced thanks to the contrasting flavors. The freshness of the peach salsa mitigates some of the heat in the pork rub.

2 pork tenderloins

Chipotle Brown Sugar Rub

2 Tablespoons cumin
1 Tablespoon chipotle chili powder
1 Tablespoon salt
1 Tablespoon ground black pepper
1½ teaspoons ground coriander
½ teaspoon ground cayenne pepper
1 Tablespoon brown sugar

Peach Salsa

3 ripe peaches, diced
½ jalapeno, seeded and minced
½ red bell pepper, diced
3–4 scallions, minced
2 Tablespoons cilantro, chopped
Zest and juice of 1 lime
½ teaspoon curry powder
1½ teaspoons honey
1 teaspoon rice-wine vinegar

Mix the chipotle brown sugar rub, coat the pork evenly with it, and grill until done. To produce pork that is moist and tender, briefly sear the outside at high heat on the grill, then cook for about 30 minutes on the lowest possible setting. After letting it rest a bit, slice the tenderloin into medallions.

Serve topped with the fresh peach salsa made by simply combining the ingredients listed above.

Serves 8.

Adapted from a recipe by Ports Cafe in Geneva, NY.

Tomato & Peach Sauce for Fish

This is a delectable summer sauce that will enhance any fresh fish or scallops you pour it over. Make sure to cook the fennel and shallots well in the beginning, as they will not have much additional time after their initial cooking to become soft and tender (which is how you want them!). You can leave the sauce chunky or do a final purée after all ingredients have been combined on the stovetop.

2 fresh ripe peaches
1 small ripe tomato
Splash of olive oil
1 small shallot, finely diced
½ bulb of fresh fennel, diced
¼ cup dry white wine
1 Tablespoon butter
1 teaspoon fresh fennel greens, chopped

Remove the skins and the pits from the peaches, core the tomatoes, and put both into a blender or food processor and purée until smooth. Set aside.

In a small saucepan, heat some olive oil. Add the chopped shallots and fennel bulb and sauté until the shallot is translucent. Add wine and then cook off about half the liquid.

Next, add to the saucepan ½ cup of the peach and tomato purée (you can freeze any leftovers for another time). Simmer for 5 minutes. Remove from heat and whisk in the butter and chopped fennel greens. Promptly pour over seared scallops, grilled salmon, or any white fish.

Makes approximately 2 cups.

Adapted from a recipe by Stonecat Cafe in Hector, NY.

Butternut & Chèvre Pudding

This is a lovely fall dish—richly orange. Though it is mostly made up of squash, do not conceive of this as a light vegetable casserole. It is deliciously dense and creamy and salty—a real cool-weather treat. It may be best served with just a simple green salad.

> 4 cups butternut squash purée, as prepared below
> 6 eggs
> 3 cups milk
> 1½ cups semolina flour
> 2 Tablespoons chopped herbs
>   (equal amounts of rosemary, thyme, and sage)
> 2 Tablespoons salt
> 10½ ounces chèvre (goat cheese), crumbled

Begin by roasting two or three squash, halved, seeded, and placed cut-side down on a baking sheet in a 350-degree oven for about an hour. When a knife easily pierces the flesh, it is ready. Let it cool, then scoop out the squash and purée in a food processor.

When you are ready to make the pudding, combine all of the ingredients, minus the chèvre, in a large bowl and mix until well combined. Then fold in the chèvre.

The pudding can be baked in individual-serving bowls, or in one large baking dish. Bake at 350 degrees for between 25 and 50 minutes (depending on the pan size), until it has become firm in the center.

Serves 8–10.

Adapted from a recipe by Next Door Bar & Grill in Pittsford, NY.

The Greenest Grocer

With headquarters in Rochester, New York, at the center of the Finger Lakes region, and a growing network of stores that stretches across the Northeast, Wegmans is now widely considered the finest grocer in America. In 2009, 32,000 shoppers answering a Consumer Reports survey placed the company number one in the nation for the quality of its fruits, vegetables, meats, and other foodstuffs.

Wegmans puts a heavy emphasis on fresh produce, and on local sourcing in particular. It works closely with growers near its stores to achieve consistent standards of high quality, and then promotes the local farmers and their products by name.

In 2007, Wegmans even founded its own organic research farm near one of the Finger Lakes to explore growing techniques and different plant varieties. The harvests from the company farm are sold in its Rochester-area stores. (During the week these words are being written the farm is shipping early cherry and grape tomatoes from 1,104 plants in 13 varieties.)

The company was also a pioneer in establishing restaurant-quality Market Cafés right inside Wegmans groceries. These are now large operations that sell gourmet ready-to-eat meals, including many international foods, for consumption on the premises or at home.

Wegmans has founded several freestanding restaurants as well. The latest is a high-end grill in suburban Rochester called Next Door Bar & Grill, which features produce from the Wegmans organic farm and other local products. The facility includes a large test kitchen where executive chef Chris Brandt and guest restaurateurs experiment with different foods and menus, offer cooking demonstrations and lectures, bring in focus groups to garner consumer feedback, test food and wine pairings, and host parties and special events. Several recipes from Next Door Bar & Grill are included in this book.

Halibut in Pea Sauce

This is a mild, moist, uncomplicated way to prepare fish. The texture is nice, the soft green color is attractive, and there is no strong fishy flavor for eaters to object to. You could substitute other types of fish, but the halibut works exceptionally well.

1 teaspoon garlic, minced
1 teaspoon shallots, minced
1 Tablespoon olive oil
2 cups half and half
1½ cups fresh or frozen peas
Salt and pepper to taste
4–6 fresh halibut fillets

Preheat oven to 400 degrees.

Begin by making the pea sauce. Sauté the garlic and shallots in a small saucepan for a few minutes in half of the oil, then add the half and half and let it come to a simmer. Next add the peas, salt, and pepper, and bring back to a simmer; cook for about two minutes. Purée in a blender and set aside.

Pour the olive oil in a frying pan and bring to fairly high heat. Place the halibut in the pan and sear for a few minutes on each side. The goal is to quickly create some brown crunchy crust, without burning.

Then transfer the fillets into an oven pan, pour the hot pea sauce over the fish, and place pan in oven. Bake for 10 minutes.

Serves 4–6.

Adapted from a recipe by Veraisons Restaurant in Dundee, NY.

Cilantro Shrimp Risotto

Risotto is a versatile and fun food because it can be flavored with virtually anything. You can throw in whatever vegetables you have on hand, any kind of cheese, or whichever herbs are currently in your garden or refrigerator. This recipe is full-bodied, and filling enough to make a meal with one of the vegetable side dishes featured in this book, like Brussels Sprouts Confetti, page 138.

2 Tablespoons olive oil
½ cup shallots, sliced
1 Tablespoon garlic, minced
2 cups arborio (or similar) rice
½ cup vermouth (or any dry white wine)
3 cups chicken broth
1¼ cup clam juice
1 pound peeled raw shrimp
Salt and pepper to taste
1⅛ cup heavy cream
½ cup Asiago cheese, grated
1 Tablespoon cilantro, chopped
Juice of 1 lemon

In a large heavy-bottomed pot, heat the oil and sauté the shallots and garlic. Stir the rice into the hot oil to coat every grain. When you can start to smell the aroma of toasting rice, add the vermouth and cook until the pot is dry again.

Add the chicken broth in three doses, stirring continually. Wait until the stock is absorbed before adding more. At this point your rice should begin to look "creamy."

Add the clam juice, shrimp, salt, and pepper. Stir the mixture well while it simmers and starts to thicken.

Finish the risotto with the cream, Asiago, cilantro, and lemon, combining thoroughly and adding more salt and pepper if needed.

Serves 6–8.

Adapted from a recipe by Next Door Bar & Grill in Pittsford, NY.

Spinach & Feta Quiche

This is the rock-solid basic quiche recipe that we return to over and over in our family. We've never found another version quite this satisfying. Our family's pie crust, passed down through many generations, makes this extra special.

> One 9-inch unbaked pie shell
> 6 cups fresh spinach leaves
> 6–8 fresh basil leaves, chopped
> (or ½ teaspoon or so of dried basil)
> 1 cup feta cheese, crumbled
> 2 cups cheddar cheese, grated
> 1 Tablespoon flour
> 4 eggs
> 1½ cups whole milk

First make your pie crust—see page 166. You may want to halve that recipe, as you need only a bottom crust. Or, double this recipe and make two quiches.

Preheat oven to 400 degrees. Steam spinach and drain well. Spread the spinach on the bottom of the pie shell and sprinkle with chopped basil. In a medium bowl, mix the cheeses with the flour and spread over the spinach. Whisk the eggs thoroughly, add milk, and pour over the spinach and cheese. Bake for 15 minutes, then lower the heat to 325 degrees and bake for another 25 to 30 minutes, until lightly browned.

Serves 6.

*Adapted from **Horn of the Moon Cookbook,** by Ginny Callan.*

Black Beans & Coconut Rice with Mango Salsa

This entirely vegetarian recipe is bursting with flavor. If you can possibly find it in a specialty foods store, use the coconut oil—it has a butter-like consistency and a beautiful fresh aroma and taste. You can substitute white rice for brown, but make sure you don't skip the mango salsa. The combination of its chilliness against the hot beans, and its sweetness against other spiciness, makes it the essential fulcrum of the dish. This is a memorable concoction created by one of America's most re-nowned vegetarian restaurants.

Beans

1½ cups chopped onions
3 garlic cloves, minced
2 Tablespoons olive oil
1 Tablespoon fresh ginger root, grated
1 teaspoon fresh thyme (or ½ teaspoon dried)
½ teaspoon ground allspice
3 16-ounce cans of black beans, drained
¾ cup orange juice
Salt, ground black pepper, and Tabasco sauce to taste

Sauté the onions and garlic in the oil until the onions begin to soften. Add the ginger, thyme, and allspice, and stir until the onions are very soft. Add the beans and orange juice and cook on low heat for about 15 minutes, stirring occasionally, until the mixture thickens slightly (mashing some beans with the back of a spoon for a thicker consistency). Add salt, pepper, and Tabasco.

Rice

2 cups brown rice (or white), uncooked
1½ teaspoons turmeric
½ cup unsweetened coconut flakes
2½ Tablespoons coconut oil
    (may substitute other vegetable oil)
4 cups water
½ stick cinnamon

Sauté the rice, turmeric, and coconut flakes in the oil for 2 to 3 minutes. Stir constantly to coat everything with the oil. Add the water and the cinnamon stick. Bring the water to a boil, then reduce heat and simmer for about 40 minutes or until the water has been absorbed (white rice will cook a bit faster). Remove from the heat and allow rice to sit for 10 minutes, then gently fluff.

Salsa

> 2 ripe mangoes, or frozen mango chunks
>   (may substitute pineapple, papaya, or cantaloupe)
> 1 small cucumber, peeled and diced
> 1 tomato, diced
> Juice of 1 lime
> Salt to taste
> ½ of a fresh jalapeno pepper, minced
> 1 Tablespoon fresh cilantro, chopped

Peel and dice the mangoes. In a large bowl, mix together the mangoes, cucumber, tomato, lime juice, salt, jalapeno, and cilantro. Let the salsa sit for at least 20 minutes to allow the flavors to marry. Will keep refrigerated for a couple of days.

To serve, make a bed of rice, cover with beans, and spoon a large dollop of salsa on top.

Serves 4–6.

Adapted from a recipe by Moosewood Restaurant in Ithaca, NY.

Seared Scallops with Shallot Purée

Scallops sometimes get a bad rap for being chewy or spongy, but if you buy them fresh and follow the directions below you will be pleasantly surprised. The key is not to overcook them, and to start with a very hot pan so that the scallops get a nice crunchy, seared exterior. You may want to serve on a bed of rice, or with wheat berries, as recommended below.

2 cloves garlic, minced
3 shallots, diced
1 red bell pepper, roughly cut
1 cup vegetable stock
Salt and pepper to taste
1 Tablespoon olive oil
12 fresh sea scallops

Place the garlic, shallots, red pepper, and stock in a pot and bring to a boil. Reduce to a simmer and cook for 10 minutes. Then purée in a food processor or blender, season to taste, and set aside.

To cook the scallops, heat olive oil in a shallow pan until quite hot. Add scallops and cook for only 2 minutes on each side. If the oil is hot enough, they should be golden brown on both sides.

Serve covered with a few spoonfuls of the purée made earlier.

The Mirbeau chef recommends serving this with steamed or sautéed swiss chard, and wheat berries (cook in water, and when they are softened through, drain and stir in a bit of vegetable stock, some butter, salt and pepper, and a handful of fresh herbs—basil and parsley are lovely).

Serves 4.

Adapted from a recipe by Mirbeau Inn in Skaneateles, NY.

Roasted Red Pepper & Chive Polenta

We had given up on polenta after one bad, hours-long, lumpy experience in our kitchen. This recipe, though, is easy and quick, requires only one pot, and has twice the flavor of run-of-the-mill recipes.

Polenta tends to be a side dish in restaurants, but this version is hearty enough to center a meal around. Or serve as an accompaniment to pork or lamb. For variety, you could drizzle hot tomato sauce over it and serve with a side of steamed spinach or a salad. Or try adding cooked greens or bacon pieces right into this recipe.

1 cup chicken stock
1 cup heavy cream
½ cup polenta or fine cornmeal
¼ cup white cheddar cheese, grated
¼ cup roasted red peppers, diced
1 Tablespoon butter
1 Tablespoon fresh chives, chopped
Salt and pepper to taste

Place chicken stock and heavy cream in a medium pot and bring up to a low boil. Then whisk in the cornmeal and grated cheddar cheese. Reduce the heat to low and cook until the polenta is creamy—about 4 to 5 minutes.

Turn the heat off and stir in the roasted peppers, butter, and chives, and season to taste. Serve right away or keep warm until ready to eat. If you are going to hold the polenta for some time, be sure to cover so it doesn't form a skin.

Serves 4.

Adapted from a recipe by Rosalie's Cucina in Skaneateles, NY.

Great Meats

O.K., even if you're an unapologetic carnivore, have you ever walked into a butcher's shop or meat section and said "Oh my goodness, this place smells wonderful!"? Probably not.

Yet there's one place where this happens to us every single time we visit: the Liehs & Steigerwald family-owned butcher shop that has been located in Syracuse, New York, for 75 years. The Syracuse-to-Buffalo corridor of New York state has long been considered heaven for German sausages and meats, and L&S is the best of the best.

The place looks just like it did in the '30s; squint your eyes and you'll see men in fedoras, and cars out front shaped like melted ice sculptures. In addition to gorgeous fresh meats of all sorts, Liehs & Steigerwald handmakes 35 different kinds of sausages. They smoke their own lean bacon that will ruin you on ever again eating the stuff in the plastic wrapper. Their breakfast links are meaty and spicy, and don't melt into a puddle of fat like standard grocery-case alternatives.

They create 18 different flavors of bratwurst right on the premises, as well as bockwurst, knockwurst, and four types of liverwurst. They also make six varieties of homemade Italian sausage (sweet, mild, hot, extra hot, festival, smoked). They pickle eggs and cucumbers, make divine German potato salad, cure homemade pastrami, and even corn their own beef. Oh yeah, they'll also sharpen your knives.

Amidst this bounty of no-preservative, no-filler, all-fresh goodness, the greatest contribution made to American eating by Liehs & Steigerwald may be their home-made frankfurters. This simple American favorite is not so simple here: beef, veal, pork, and natural spices are blended, then hickory smoked. They have more peppery bite than the bland wieners most of us know, and are unforgettable. Acclaimed food critic David Rosengarten rated them the number one hot dog in America.

We buy 10 pounds of franks at a time. They freeze beautifully and can be pulled out for grilling or boiling at your convenience over a period of months. If you can't stop by L&S, our Resources section lists another upstate maker who will ship good German franks, Coneys, and sausages.

We Americans love the one-stop convenience of the mega-grocery store. But for truly wonderful, in-a-class-by-themselves meats, there is no substitute for a quality butcher shop. One of our fond hopes is that old-time meat markets will someday make the same kind of comeback that farmer's markets have experienced over the past couple decades. Search one out in your area; your palate will thank you.

Feast Lamb with White Beans

For such simplicity of ingredients and procedure, this dish is tremendously flavorful. And fragrant—cook with your windows shut and be tantalized all day!

Family members beg for this meal around holidays. (We adapted it from a delightful book of recipes celebrating the Christian calendar.) Everyone loves the beans cooked directly with the lamb. They absorb the meat juices and become tender, succulent, and explosively savory. By building layers of flavor in both the lamb and the beans, the rosemary and garlic create depth and continuity throughout the dish.

Roast

1 leg of lamb, 6–8 pounds

Juice of 1 lemon

2 Tablespoons fresh rosemary (or 2 teaspoons dried)

½ Tablespoon salt

½ teaspoon black pepper

4 cloves garlic, peeled and cut into slivers

Seasoned Beans

5 cans of cannellini beans, drained
  (or one pound of dried beans, cooked and drained)

2 cloves garlic, diced

1 small onion, chopped

1 Tablespoon fresh rosemary (or 1 teaspoon dried)

½ Tablespoon salt

½ teaspoon black pepper

Trim some of the excess fat from the leg of lamb and let the meat sit at room temperature for a half hour. Then sprinkle all over with lemon juice and rub it with salt, pepper, and rosemary. Cut small gashes into the roast with a sharp pointed knife and insert numerous slivers of garlic.

Place roast in a large pan (make sure there is a fair amount of room around the meat) and cook at 350 degrees.

Mix the beans with the garlic, onion, rosemary, salt, and pepper. At about the 90-minute mark of the roasting, pour the seasoned beans right into the pan all around the roast. Stir in with the lamb juices and return to oven for an additional half-hour of cooking.

Dish will be done after a total of about two hours of roasting. For accurate gauging, leave a meat thermometer in the center of the roast, visible through your oven door: the internal temperature will register 135 degrees for rare meat, 145 for medium-rare, and 160 for medium-well (don't overcook).

Serves 8–10.

Adapted from **A Continual Feast,** *by Evelyn Birge Vitz.*

Maple Mustard Salmon

⅔ cup melted butter
½ teaspoon dried dill
½ cup maple syrup
¼ cup Dijon-style mustard
Salt and pepper to taste
4–6 salmon fillets for grilling or broiling

Blend the first five ingredients over low heat until melted together. Pat salmon fillets dry with a paper towel then baste liberally. Continue to baste fish with sauce as it grills or broils. Turn once. Serve when fish is flaky.

Serves 4–6.

Yorkshire Pudding (with Roast Beef)

Nourishing and heart-warming as only such an old-time food can be, Yorkshire pudding with roast beef is a perfect holiday dinner. Do not fear in the least that your guests will find it dated. Since at this point most Americans have never eaten Yorkshire pudding, the novelty factor alone will keep people fascinated. And executed well, the flavor of this dish will leave your eaters too enthralled, and busy with their fork and knife, to even mutter a word.

If you can possibly get your hands on a Leihs & Steigerwald roast beef (see Great Meats on page 84), we strongly urge you to do so. If you're not in the region, seek out a butcher in your area who knows his craft. Major beef dishes like this depend entirely on the quality of the meat, and you will not regret tracking down a well-finished, high-flavor roast.

1½ cups milk
1 cup flour
2 eggs
1 teaspoon salt

First, prepare a fairly large roast beef. We will not include instructions for that here. If you need help, consult your *Joy of Cooking,* local butcher, or grandmother on preparation and cooking time.

But make sure to cook your beef in a heavy, good-sized pan with reasonable sides on it—because after you are done roasting, the pudding will rise and be baked directly in the beef drippings.

In a medium bowl, make a paste with the milk and flour. Add the eggs one at a time and beat with a fork. Stir in the salt.

As soon as your roast is done, remove it onto a platter, cover with foil, and position near oven to keep warm. Then pour the pudding batter directly into the hot beef drippings left in the roasting pan and bake at 400 degrees for 20 to 30 minutes, until puffy and golden. As it nears completion, slice roast.

The pudding will rise and then collapse back on itself, leaving a puffy, air-filled, savory shell. Cut the crunchy result into separate portions for each guest, and serve alongside the carved meat.

Serves 6.

The Ghost Deer

When nearly 10,000 acres of remote farmland in the Finger Lakes were set aside in 1941 to be used as a storage site for military ordnance, including tactical nuclear weapons, the high-security site was ringed by high fences. As the perimeter of the Seneca Army Depot was sealed, some deer ended up inside the fence.

Occasionally, a rare recessive gene will cause a normal deer to have an entirely snow-white coat. When this happens in the wild, that easily observed animal normally becomes quick prey to predators or hunters. In 1949, an all-white buck and fawn were spotted at the Seneca Army Depot—among the small deer herd living inside the fence.

Protected from hunters by the secure environment, the white deer thrived. Today, it's estimated that 200 to 300 of the deer on this reservation (now closed as a military facility, but still fenced off) are of the striking all-white variety. That makes this the largest group of white deer in the world, and when they are spotted from Route 96A or some other local road they make for a dramatic sight.

Hunt Stew

If your hunt has already succeeded, you can make this as a venison stew. If, instead, you're seeking something hearty before heading out to stalk your deer (or other challenge), then this can alternatively be made with beef. Whatever the occasion, this is likely to rank as the tastiest stew you've eaten, with lots of meat and root vegetables. It is especially welcome on any rainy or snowy day.

2 Tablespoons squash-seed or olive oil
¼ pound bacon, chopped into pieces
½ cup flour
1¼ teaspoon salt
1 teaspoon white pepper
3 pounds of venison or stew beef
   (beef chuck works well), cut into
    1-inch cubes; half venison and half
    beef is nice, too
2 cups onion, cut coarsely
2–3 cloves of garlic, minced
3 large carrots, peeled and cut into
   ½-inch slices
3 parsnips, peeled and cut into
   ½-inch slices
1 cup celery, cut into 1-inch pieces
Small rutabaga, cut into 1-inch cubes
3 bay leaves
4 cups of good quality beef stock
½ teaspoon thyme
3 good-sized potatoes,
   cut into 1-inch cubes with skin on
1 bottle lager beer
1 cup or so of green onions, chopped
   including full stem

Cut up all the meat and vegetables in advance.

Place a large stockpot over medium heat and add oil and bacon.

In a large mixing bowl, stir together flour, salt, and white pepper, then toss the venison or beef in the mixture until fully coated. Once the bacon starts to melt, add the cubed meat and sauté, stirring often. Once meat is browned and bacon begins to crisp, add onion, garlic, carrots, parsnips, celery, rutabaga, and bay leaves. Sauté about 5 minutes.

Then add beef stock, thyme, and potatoes, and bring stew to a boil. Reduce heat to low simmer, add the beer and green onions. Cover and simmer for 1½ hours, stirring often. Then remove from heat, adjust seasonings to taste, discard bay leaves.

Re-warm just before serving. Present in a bowl, perhaps with a slice of good bread. If you really want a meal that sticks to you all day, ladle over a bed of rice, egg noodles, garlic mashed potatoes, kasha, or other starch.

Serves 8.

Adapted from a recipe created by vineyard chef William Cornelius; from **Finger Lakes Wine Country** *magazine.*

Spiedies

From New York's Finger Lakes region south to the Pennsylvania border, grilled meat sandwiches called "spiedies" (SPEE-dees) are a local obsession. In Binghamton, there is even an annual three-day weekend in August where 100,000 strolling visitors sample hundreds of variations of this local food favorite. Introduced by Italian immigrants in the 1930s (In Italian a *spiedo* is a "spit" used for roasting.), spiedies were originally made of lamb. Today they are prepared using many meats (leg of lamb, pork tenderloin, top round beef steak, or local venison for example), but boneless and skinless chicken breasts are probably the favorite for home cooking.

The marinade is the key to the flavor, and there seem to be as many variations in marinade as there are taste buds on a tongue. As you get hooked on these grilled treats, feel free to adapt to your own preferences. Here is the basic recipe.

2 pounds of meat cut into 1½"–1¾" cubes
1 cup grape-seed or olive oil
¾ cup red-wine vinegar
¼ cup fresh lemon juice
2 Tablespoons honey
4 cloves garlic, minced
1 bay leaf
1½ teaspoons each dried thyme, basil, and oregano
   (double the dried amounts if using fresh herbs)
¼ teaspoon cayenne pepper
½ teaspoon black pepper
½ teaspoon salt
1 loaf Italian bread, thickly sliced
Grilling skewers

In a large bowl, combine oil, vinegar, lemon juice, and honey. Add garlic and all herbs and seasonings; stir until well blended.

Place prepared meat in a large container with a sealable lid, or a zippable plastic bag set in a shallow dish. Pour marinade over meat, and leave in refrigerator for at least 24 hours, up to three days—turning mixture a couple times per day to marinate evenly.

Two or three hours before grilling, let the mixture stand at room temperature. Then drain, saving some marinade for basting.

Preheat barbecue grill. Thread about four meat cubes on each skewer. Place

them on hot grill and cook 8 to 10 minutes, basting once or twice in the first minutes. Grill to personal preference, but avoid overcooking—moistness is a critical part of what people love about spiedies.

To serve, simply take a thick slice of Italian bread, lay a meat skewer in its center, and, using the bread as a mitt, pull cubes off skewer—the result will be a handy sandwich.

Serves 6.

Venison Spiedies

A lot of deer meat gets harvested each year from the rolling hills and woods of the Finger Lakes, and spiedies are a favorite way to consume venison. If you are a hunter or have a local source of venison, try your deer meat marinated and grilled spiedie-style. You may prepare it exactly as listed in the standard Spiedies recipe, or substitute this marinade that has evolved specifically for venison.

> ½ cup squash-seed or olive oil
> ½ cup soy sauce
> 4 Tablespoons ketchup
> 2 teaspoons Worcestershire sauce
> 4 cloves garlic, minced
> 10 bay leaves
> 4 teaspoons dried Italian herbs
>   (thyme, oregano, basil)
> 1 teaspoon dried tarragon
> ½ teaspoon dried sage
> 2 teaspoons red hot sauce

Follow preparation directions for standard spiedies. Discard the bay leaves after marinating is complete. This sauce will marinate about two pounds of venison.

Serves 6.

Muffaletta Sandwich

Only available as a special, you can sometimes get a great version of this New Orleans favorite (as well as other marvelous dishes) at The Village Tavern right on the town square in Hammondsport—the historic center of New York winemaking. We're not sure what vintage we'd order to go with this spicy two-hander, but we know the Tavern would have one that's right—because they stock a breadth of local wines sufficient to win the Wine Spectator's Award of Excellence every year since 1995.

What really makes this sandwich special is the tanginess of the olive relish—we strongly suggest you make extra relish to spoon onto other things, and nibble on its own. It's that delicious! This sandwich is filling and would be ideal for a weeknight dinner, or of course for lunch any day.

½ cup pitted calamata olives, diced fine

½ cup green olives, diced fine

½ cup pitted black olives, diced fine

¼ cup carrots, diced fine

¼ cup red onion, diced fine

¼ cup celery, diced fine

¼ cup red bell pepper, diced fine

¼ cup garlic cloves, diced fine

Main Dishes

½ cup olive oil

1 Tablespoon crushed red pepper

½ pound deli-sliced mortadella

½ pound deli-sliced Capicola ham

½ pound deli-sliced genoa salami

½ pound deli-sliced provolone cheese

1 sheet focaccia bread cut into 4-inch squares
   (or Kaiser rolls, or any sort of hearty sandwich bread)

First, make the olive relish. Combine the chopped olives, carrots, onion, celery, bell pepper, garlic, olive oil, and crushed red pepper. Cover and refrigerate for at least three hours. This relish can be kept in the refrigerator for up to three weeks if sealed well.

When you are ready to make the sandwiches, preheat oven to 350 degrees and line a baking pan with aluminum foil. Slice the bread in half and lay crust sides down on the baking pan. Spoon the olive relish generously onto both top and bottom of the bread (depending on your taste you may want more or less). Add two slices each of the mortadella, Capicola, and salami to the bottom of each sandwich. Next add one slice of provolone cheese to both the top and bottom of the bread. Bake for 20 minutes.

After removing from oven, place the top and bottom together, and slice in half. Makes 4–6 sandwiches.

Adapted from a recipe by The Village Tavern in Hammondsport, NY.

Cornell Chicken

This is a local food icon in the Finger Lakes region. Its creator, Robert Baker, was an animal science professor at Cornell who sought ways, throughout his career, to increase chicken consumption. (Among other things, he invented the process for making frozen chicken nuggets.)

This simple—but pungent—recipe for marinating chicken prior to barbecuing was his most personal contribution to increasing the popularity of poultry in America. What is known as "Cornell Chicken" quickly became a huge hit throughout central New York, then spread far beyond.

It is hard to describe Cornell Chicken unless you've had it—particularly because the ingredients are pretty pedestrian. The cider vinegar is probably the crucial element, adding both tang and tenderness. The end result is stronger flavored and moister than typical barbecued chicken, especially if you plan ahead and let the chicken sit in the marinade for several hours before grilling.

This is our number one summer grilling choice, and we hope that it will become yours, too.

By the way, should you ever visit the delightful New York State Fair in August, you can get Cornell Chicken grilled by the inventor's own family at Baker's Chicken Shack—wedged between the Poultry Barn and the Tilt-a-Whirl.

1 egg
½ cup vegetable oil
1 cup apple-cider vinegar

1½ Tablespoon salt
½ Tablespoon poultry seasoning
½ teaspoon black pepper
8–10 chicken breasts or 4 broiling halves

First, beat the egg in a small bowl. (Now you know the egg does indeed come first, before the chicken.) Add the oil and whisk thoroughly. Add the rest of the ingredients, except for the chicken, and stir or shake well to emulsify.

Rinse the chicken in running water, pat dry with a paper towel, and immerse in the marinade—ideally in a tight-sealing container you can flip or rotate periodically. Marinate your chicken for at least a couple of hours before grilling. (But don't leave it more than about 24 hours, and keep the container in the refrigerator throughout.)

As always, don't overgrill chicken or you'll make it tough and dry.

Makes enough marinade for the meat of up to two chickens.

Curried Chicken Salad
with Pomegranate Seeds

A perfect way to use surplus grilled or roasted chicken. Or just poach several raw chicken breasts in water with a pinch of herbs, salt, and pepper; they'll be cooked through after simmering for 10 minutes. Then make the salad.

3–4 chicken breasts, cooked
½ cup slivered almonds or cracked walnuts
½ cup raisins or dried cranberries
2 celery stalks, chopped
1 can (approx. 11 ounces) mandarin oranges
⅓ cup pomegranate seeds
½ cup mayonnaise
2–4 teaspoons curry powder (to taste)
Salt and pepper to taste

Place cubed or shredded cooked chicken in a large bowl. Add the nuts, raisins/cranberries, celery, mandarin oranges, and pomegranate seeds. Stir gently.

Mix curry powder into the mayonnaise, then dress the chicken mixture with the curried mayo. Add salt and pepper—and more curry if needed.

Serve the salad on a bed of fresh greens.

Serves 4–6 people as a light main course.

Family-Reunion Ham

Here is a spectacular holiday treat with real table appeal—the glaze adds not only deeper flavor but also a handsome gloss. The ham is moist and succulent due to the time it simmers in the fragrant liquid. Leftovers can be used in sandwiches, or grilled to accompany eggs in the morning.

6–7 pound picnic-shoulder ham, bone-in

1 gallon water

1 bottle red wine

4 bay leaves

2 cinnamon sticks

1 Tablespoon cardamon seeds

1 Tablespoon whole cloves

Glaze

8–12 ounces red or black currant jam

1½ teaspoons ground cinnamon

1½ teaspoons smoked paprika

1 Tablespoon red-wine vinegar

Unwrap the ham and place in a large pot. If there is a netting, leave it on, as it makes it easier to turn the ham while boiling. Add the water, wine, and seasonings, and simmer on medium heat for two hours, turning once. Then remove ham from pot, drain, cut off netting, and place on an oven-proof tray or platter.

As the ham approaches the end of its boiling period, make the glaze. In a sauce-pan, combine the jam, cinnamon, smoked paprika, and vinegar over medium heat.

Once the ham has been transferred to the oven tray, spoon half of the glaze over the meat and place under the broiler in the oven until the fat starts to crackle. Glaze a second time and return to the broiler. Take care not to burn the ham at this point. When it is nice and crispy, remove the ham and carve on a carving board.

Serves 8–10.

Adapted from a recipe by Simply Red Bistro in Ovid, NY.

Dinosaur BBQ Sauce

Dinosaur Bar-B-Que began as a towed-behind-the-van mobile concession that specialized in motorcycle gatherings and fairs. The road-weary owners eventually opened a restaurant in Syracuse, which instantly became standing-room-only thanks to great food, fast and sassy service, smoking music, and modest prices. Soon there was another joint on the opposite edge of the Finger Lakes region, in Rochester, and today there are five locations, including one in Harlem. A full rack of national awards suggests the place purveys the best BBQ in America, and it all starts with their base sauce—which the proprietors have kindly allowed us to reproduce below. A balance of sweet, savor, and spice, you can slather this on all the ribs, chicken, and pork you grill up in your own backyard.

2 Tablespoons olive oil

½ cup minced onion

¼ cup minced green pepper

½ jalapeno pepper, seeded and minced

1 Tablespoon minced garlic

1 pinch salt

1 pinch black pepper

1 small can (approx. 16 ounces) diced tomatoes

1 cup ketchup

½ cup water

⅓ cup Worcestershire sauce

¼ cup cider vinegar

2 Tablespoons lemon juice

2 Tablespoons molasses

2 Tablespoons cayenne pepper sauce

2 Tablespoons spicy brown mustard

⅓ cup dark brown sugar, packed

½ Tablespoon chili powder

1 teaspoon ground black pepper

¼ teaspoon ground allspice

Pour the oil into a large saucepan over medium-high heat. After oil has heated, add the onions, green peppers, jalapeno, garlic, salt, and pepper, and stir until vegetables soften.

Add remaining ingredients and bring to a boil, then lower the heat so the sauce simmers. Simmer for 10 minutes.

Let the sauce cool, then pour into a sealable container that can be stored in the fridge until ready for use.

Makes 4 cups.

Adapted from a recipe by Dinosaur Bar-B-Que in Syracuse, NY.

Tomato Cobbler

This tomato cobbler is so divine it is actually one prominent reason we look forward to summer and the arrival of fresh tomato season. Yet it is tremendously simple to make. As soon as you can squirrel away a few heirloom tomatoes fresh off the vine, do yourself a favor and cook this up. With only a light green salad and a glass of white wine or iced tea, we predict it will be your favorite meal of the summer.

2 cups flour
4 teaspoons baking powder
1 stick cold butter, cut into cubes
¾ cup milk
2 pounds fresh tomatoes (roughly two very large
   fruits, or 4–5 smaller ones)
2 Tablespoons fresh basil, chopped
Salt and pepper to taste
2 cups sharp cheddar cheese, grated, divided
⅔ cup mayonnaise
Juice of half a lemon

First make the biscuit-dough crust: Mix the flour and baking powder and then cut the butter into the dry ingredients using a pastry cutter or fork. Add the milk and mix (do not overmix). Take about half of the dough and pat it into the bottom of a 9-inch pie pan.

Slice the tomatoes, and layer them over the bottom crust. Add the chopped basil, salt and pepper, and 1 cup of the grated cheese. Stir together the mayonnaise and lemon juice and drizzle over the cheese. Sprinkle the rest of the cheese on top and then cover with the remaining dough, in pieces, for a rustic look.

Bake at 400 degrees for about 25 minutes, until golden, and let sit for a few minutes before serving. Always serve warm or reheat before serving.

Makes one large 9-inch cobbler.

Almond/Cashew Chicken Salad

If you're tired of other favorite chicken salads, this nutty, spicy, sweet-salty alternative might be a welcome change. Nut butter sources can be found in our Resources section.

5–6 chicken breasts, cooked and cubed
¼ cup peanut oil
⅓ cup soy sauce
⅓ cup cider vinegar
⅓ cup honey
¾ teaspoon cayenne pepper
⅓ cup almond or cashew butter
½ cup chopped green onions
¼ cup chopped almonds or cashews
Lettuce, or green pepper slices, and kaiser rolls

Cook chicken and cut into bite-sized cubes. In a medium frying pan, heat peanut oil, soy sauce, vinegar, honey, pepper, and nut butter, stirring until fully combined and smooth. Stir in green onions, nuts, and chicken, then stir to coat all well.

Serve warm or cold atop a bed of lettuce, or on a kaiser roll with green pepper slices. The flavors will meld and deepen the next day, so embrace leftovers.

Serves 6–8.

Arugula Pesto

This is a departure from the classic basil pesto. Instead of the famed aromatic herb, it uses arugula—which gives the end product an extra bite, almost a bitterness, that makes for a nice variation.

Pesto-making can be fun—because the recipe doesn't have to be followed to the "T." You can add more or less of the flavors you particularly love, and adjust for the individual character of the ingredients you've got that day. That is true of a lot of cooking, but with pesto, improvisation will almost always turn out well—so long as you wield high-quality versions of the half-dozen basic ingredients you're spinning up and down, and employing your taste buds as you go.

4 cups arugula
2 cups baby spinach
2 ounces pine nuts, toasted on a dry skillet
½ cup Parmesan or Romano cheese, grated
2 cloves garlic, peeled, or garlic scapes
Juice of about half a lemon
½ cup olive oil
Salt and pepper to taste

Combine all ingredients in the food processor and purée until smooth.

Serve over your favorite pasta as a meal. Or use as a garnish on sandwiches, or with meats or seafood.

Makes 2 cups.

Adapted from a recipe by Rosalie's Cucina in Skaneateles, NY.

Salads
& Side Dishes

You can count the seeds in an apple,

but you can't count the apples in a seed.

—Upstate New York aphorism

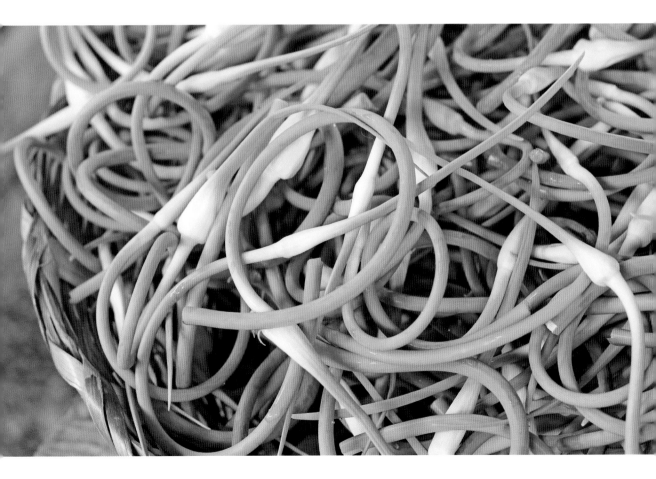

Pine-Nut Salad with Goat Cheese

Texture, color, and savory flavors abound in this unusual salad/garnish combining cooked vegetables, pine nuts, and your favorite goat cheese.

1 eggplant, peeled and cut into small cubes
2 Tablespoons olive oil
1 large red onion, diced
8 cloves garlic, diced
1 small-to-medium bag of spinach
1½ cups fresh tomato, diced
¾ cup pine nuts, toasted
15 pitted black olives (approx.), chopped
15 basil leaves (approx.)
1½ Tablespoons capers
1 cup roasted red peppers, chopped
1 cup goat cheese, crumbled
Pinch of salt
Black pepper to taste

In a large frying pan, sauté the eggplant in olive oil for 5 minutes. Then add the onion and garlic, and sauté for another 3 to 4 minutes. Finally, add the spinach and cook just until it is softened.

Place cooked mixture in a medium bowl and add all other ingredients. Salt and pepper to taste, tossing well.

Serves 5–6.

Pictured on opposite page as a garnish for grilled eggplant.

Adapted from a recipe by Cobblestone Restaurant in Geneva, NY.

Pickled Beets

Pickled beets are delicious. They're good for you. And they are beautiful served on a bed of greens with a dollop of cottage cheese or a sprinkling of feta alongside. If you are someone who finds plain beets too sweet, try this recipe. They are sharp-flavored, clean and fresh, and so soft. They can be lovely sliced into a tossed salad as well.

4 (baseball-sized) to 8
   (plum-sized) fresh beets
1 Tablespoon olive oil
1 cup cider or wine
   vinegar
1 cup water
¼ cup sugar

Preheat oven to 350 degrees.

Trim the tops off the beets, wash them, and place in a large baking pan. Sprinkle with olive oil, cover the pan tightly with aluminum foil, and pop it in the oven for one hour.

After the beets cool, remove their skins by rubbing them with a paper towel. Then slice them fairly thinly into a large marinating bowl.

In a saucepan, heat the vinegar, water, and sugar long enough to dissolve all the sugar. Pour over the sliced beets. Let sit until they reach room temperature, then refrigerate for 4 hours or more before serving.

Serve chilled. Pickled beets can be kept refrigerated in their marinade and served over many days.

Serves 4–6.

Watermelon Summer Salad

If you have doubts about the combination of watermelon and feta, they'll be cured after the first bite. Once all the flavors meld together during a brief marination in the fridge, there is hardly a more refreshing side salad than this one. Its juicy sweetness balances barbecued meats or other savory flavors.

8 cups seedless watermelon,
    scooped or cut into bite-sized cubes
¼ cup fresh mint, finely chopped
1 cup feta cheese, crumbled
¼ cup olive oil
1 teaspoon sea salt
1 teaspoon fresh ground black pepper

Toss all ingredients in a mixing bowl and allow to marinate in the refrigerator for 30 minutes. Serves 6.

Adapted from a recipe by Simply Red Bistro in Ovid, NY.

Elsie's Quinoa & Lime Salad

This healthy salad is sweet, tangy, salty, and fresh-tasting all at once. The recipe comes from a good family friend and excellent cook who has shared many satisfying dishes with us. This one is particularly adaptable. You might experiment with different vegetables, lemon instead of lime, or cooking the quinoa in chicken stock to give it extra depth and flavor.

A splash of olive oil
½ cup quinoa, uncooked
¼ teaspoon cumin
Salt
Freshly ground black pepper
1 cup water
1 large tomato, chopped
1 red pepper, chopped
2 scallions, chopped
2–3 Tablespoons chopped parsley
1 cup black beans
1 cup corn
2–3 Tablespoons fresh lime juice

Heat the olive oil in a medium saucepan and sauté the quinoa for about 30 seconds. Add the cumin, a dash of both salt and pepper, and water. Bring to a boil, then cover and let simmer until the quinoa is cooked and the water is absorbed, about 20 minutes. You will know the quinoa is done when the grain opens to reveal a curled sprout. Cool and fluff the quinoa.

Meanwhile, chop the vegetables and squeeze the lime juice. When the quinoa is cooled, combine all of the ingredients and season to taste with salt and pepper.
Serves 8–10.

Al Dente Garden Bean Salad

If you're looking for a light and refreshing summer meal, start here. The Mirbeau Inn calls this vegetable dish "spa-inspired," and when you make it you'll understand why. This is food that is nourishing enough to rejuvenate you, but also so light and fresh, it leaves you feeling healthy—like after a good workout!

1 Tablespoon olive oil
2 cups fresh green or yellow beans, snapped
1 yellow summer squash, diced
2 cloves garlic, minced
1 tomato, diced
¼ cup chives, chopped
5 large basil leaves sliced into thin strips
Salt and pepper to taste
Arugula, baby spinach, or mixed greens
Juice of 2 limes

Sauté the beans, squash, and garlic in the oil for 3 to 4 minutes. (You want to cook the vegetables only very lightly, leaving them al dente style.) Remove from heat and toss with the tomato, chives, and basil. Let the mixture stand at room temperature for an hour or two to allow the flavors to meld. Adjust with salt and pepper.

Place the arugula or whatever greens you have on a plate, top with the bean salad and squeeze fresh lime juice over all.

Shown here as the perfect side dish for Cornell Chicken (see page 96).

Serves 4.

Adapted from a recipe by Mirbeau Inn in Skaneateles, NY.

Homemade Sauerkraut

1–5 heads of fresh cabbage (depending on the size of your fermentation crock)

1 container of sea salt or pickling salt (Table salt will work but is not recommended, as it has anti-caking agents that will cloud the brine.)

1 large, wide-top crock or food-grade bucket (Many grocery bakeries will give you free food-grade buckets they receive ingredients in and then discard.)

1 plate that fits just inside your crock/bucket

A couple of clean tea towels or handkerchiefs you can use alternatingly

1 clean gallon-jug of water

Core the cabbage and shred fairly finely—using a knife (probably fastest), grater, or food processor—one head at a time. Place the shreddings from one head in your crock, sprinkle with 2 tablespoons of salt (more if it's an exceptionally large head), mix well, and tamp down hard with your fist or a wooden rolling pin or mallet. This is to compact the cabbage and begin squeezing water out of it.

Then shred another cabbage, mix into crock with another 2 tablespoons of salt, tamp hard. Continue until crock is full or you have as much as you'd like to ferment.

Wet the clean tea towel or handkerchief and spread it over the top of your final layer. Place the close-fitting plate on top of that, and weight the plate down with the 1-gallon water jug (which you are using just for weight—keep the water inside the jug).

Place crock in a closet or out-of-the-way room where the temperature is about 75 degrees. After 24 hours, the salt should have drawn enough water out of the cabbage to just cover it. If not, make a little brine (2 tablespoons of salt per quart of warm water) and just cover the shreds.

The fermentation will start almost immediately, thanks to wild yeasts in the air! Check the kraut every couple of days. Don't worry if you find a mold bloom on top—it's a normal part of the fermentation process. That's the reason for the tea towel—just lift it off, skim any mold which might remain around the edges, then put a fresh towel on top for easy mold removal next time. This keeps the mold out of the sauerkraut itself. Don't be squeamish—bread, wine, cheese, soy sauce, and other foods are all fermented!

Depending on how warm the room and how sour you like your kraut, it should be ready within 2 to 6 weeks. Just keep tasting, and when it has the amount of sourness and crunch you like, you're done!

Place the finished product in the fridge (where the flavor will continue to evolve more slowly), and dip out batches for use whenever you like. Or freeze, or can the kraut in jars, if you want to end fermentation completely and keep the kraut for longer periods.

Options: you can add some shredded red cabbage, grated carrots, turnips, or beets, or even a small amount of apple slices to add a bit of color and extra flavor to your kraut.

Sauerkraut Central

The Finger Lakes region is home to the world's largest producer of sauerkraut: the Great Lakes Kraut company of Shortsville, New York. In addition to putting cabbages in a lot of local fields, an annual Sauerkraut Festival is held in nearby Phelps, every August. A sauerkraut prince and princess are crowned, there is a kraut-eating contest, you can even go bowling with cabbage heads.

It appears that the process of fermentation makes sauerkraut even healthier than (already nutritious) raw or cooked cabbage, especially as an anti-cancer compound. Central New Yorkers buy most of their kraut chilled in fresh-packs, rather than canned, and use it lots of ways. (Including in a cake! See Chocolate Sauerkraut Cake, p.183.) Pork and sauerkraut were practically made to be cooked together. But a whole chicken is also delightful stuffed with sauerkraut and roasted.

It's actually easy to pickle homemade sauerkraut yourself—right in your kitchen, or closet, or garage. And the home-fermented variety tends to be much more flavorful, tender, and interesting than commercially produced and preserved varieties. Those of you with access to several fresh heads of cabbage, a sense of adventure, and a taste for tang, should try our old family recipe.

Four Bean Salad

This is a simple and old-fashioned side dish. No need to get fancy and trick this recipe up—the reason it has endured so long is because it works so well just as is.

1 can green beans, drained
1 can yellow beans, drained
1 can red kidney beans, drained
1 can garbanzo beans (chickpeas), drained
1 Tablespoon sweet onion, chopped
⅔ cup olive oil
1 cup apple-cider vinegar
1 cup sugar
¼ cup water
1 teaspoon salt
Freshly ground black pepper to taste

Mix all the vegetables in a large bowl that you can refrigerate with a top or plastic-wrap covering.

In a saucepan, bring the oil, vinegar, sugar, water, and salt to a boil. Pour hot liquid over bean mix and let marinate for a few hours. Season with freshly ground black pepper. Serve icy cold.

Serves 10.

Pickle Potato Salad

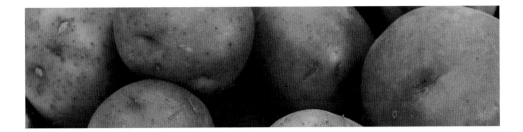

We find most potato salads to be too sweet and too mayonnaisey. This one, from our family-member Kathy, is just the opposite. The special ingredients are lots of crunchy dill pickles and (surprise!) dill-pickle juice right from the jar—which, along with the mustard, lends all the flavor. (For this recipe we much favor Claussen dill pickles, which are not cooked and thus crisper, and stored in the refrigerated case of most grocery stores.) In central New York we are spoiled with a range of delicious local potatoes, but we're sure you can find a favorite variety to use in this recipe—anything from baby reds to Yukon golds.

4–6 large potatoes
1 big serving-spoonful of mayonnaise
2 big serving-spoonfuls of sour cream
1½ Tablespoons Dijon mustard
⅓ to ½ cup dill pickle juice
3–4 large dill pickles, cut into small cubes
Salt and ground black pepper to taste

Wash the potatoes and put in a medium pot with water. We usually leave them unpeeled, but that's your choice and also depends on the freshness of the potatoes. Boil potatoes until cooked, then cut into bite-sized chunks.

In a large bowl, mix mayonnaise, sour cream, mustard, and pickle juice. Add the chopped pickles and the potato pieces. (Put the potatoes in while they are still warm, so they will soak up more flavors from the dressing.) Stir to coat. Add more or less pickle juice to get a nice consistency. You want it pretty wet. Add salt and pepper to taste.

Serve warm, or chill in the refrigerator for use later. The potatoes will eventually absorb much of the dressing and become a bit dry, so don't keep too long. Or just add more pickle juice then.

Serves 6–8.

"Golden" Apples

The perfect meal, suggested the Roman poet Horace, starts with eggs and ends with apples. Thanks to the fact that apple seeds produce rampant variations in each generation, the handful of wild apples that originated centuries ago in south Asia have now yielded literally thousands of different flavors, colors, and palate textures.

Apples have been a favorite in America from our beginnings. In 1629, the Boston Bay Company ordered apple seeds from England. By the mid-1600s, apples were an important Colonial food—eaten fresh, stored in cellars, and dried. Within a few years of the apple's arrival, many thousands of gallons of cider were being produced in America. An apple tree planted in New York by Peter Stuyvesant in 1647 was still bearing fruit when it was killed 219 years later in a train derailment.

Some of the very best apples in the world are grown in the Finger Lakes. Apart from the salubrious climate, one reason is the famous agricultural experiment station at Geneva, New York. Part of Cornell University for most of the last century, the Geneva station's breeders created beloved apple strains like the Empire, Cortland, Jonagold, Macoun, and Jonamac. A special USDA program based at Geneva is the world's greatest "bank" of apple DNA. It stores dormant buds preserved in liquid nitrogen from nearly all known varieties, including original strains of wild apple collected from Asia in seven expeditions since 1989.

The "controlled atmosphere" storage revolution (likewise developed at Cornell) slows the aging of commercial fruit after it's picked, and preserves firmness, acidity, sugars, and Vitamin C. This has made it possible to buy high-quality apples year-round. But select your vendors carefully, buy in small quantities, and always keep apples refrigerated. That apple bowl on the counter looks nice, but it is death for taste and nutrition. Even when refrigerated, apples should be eaten within two weeks of being taken out of your vendor's super-low-oxygen controlled-atmosphere storage; they will decline fast in quality. Apples are a superb source of fiber, and high in healthy antioxidants. And consider this: an 8-ounce glass of cider contains the juice of about 2½ apples.

Among the scores of superb cider and juice makers in the Finger Lakes, Red Jacket Orchards is one of the best known, due to their direct-to-consumer sales at farmer's markets throughout New York City. From their upstate orchards near Geneva, the Nicholson family trucks down fresh apples, apricots, plums, raspberries, currants, gooseberries, and other fruit, plus a wide variety of 100% fruit juices—from lemon-apple blend to Tart Cherry Stomp.

Recently, high-end hard ciders, apple wines, and apple vodka have also begun to be produced in the Finger Lakes region. Beak and Skiff, listed under Apples in the Resources section, produce several apple wines as well as an apple vodka.

On page 167 you will find a great recipe for a simple, non-gluey apple pie with marvelous fresh-from-the-orchard taste. And pie is only the beginning of what apples can do in cooking. Cobblers, crumbles, crisps, betties, buckles, tarts, grunts, and pandowdies—the possibilities are as various and tempting as the names.

Apple Yogurt Salad

This is a healthy side dish, perfect for any time of the year. We tend to make it most in the fall, when apples are in season and are especially crisp and tasty. Use any hard, tangy apples. (Empires are great.) Avoid varieties that are extra sweet or soft.

> 5 fresh apples
> A squeeze of juice from a fresh lemon
> ¾ cup raisins
> 1 cup walnuts, pecans, or almonds, chopped
> 1 cup crushed pineapple, drained
> 1 cup plain yogurt

Core the apples, cut into bite-sized chunks, place in a medium bowl, and squeeze lemon over them. Add the raisins, nuts, and pineapple. Feel free to increase or decrease the proportions of these according to taste. Add the yogurt and stir gently until combined. If you want more of a dessert dish, you may add a dollop of honey.

Serves approximately 6.

Apples for Cooking & Eating

Variety—	Characteristics—	Excellent for—				
Braeburn	Complex fruity flavor, juicy, firmest apple grown		Salad			Baking
Cortland	Sweet, sprightly, velvety, non-browning; great in salad!	Fresh	**Salad!**			
Crispin	Spicy, crunchy	Fresh				
Empire	Tart balanced with sweet, very crisp and firm	Fresh				
Fuji	Very sweet and aromatic, stores well					Baking
Gala	Sweet, granular flesh	Fresh				
Ginger Gold	Sweet, firm, slow to brown	Fresh	Salad			
Golden Delicious	Honey sweet, mild, semi-firm, juicy	Fresh				
Granny Smith	Moderately sweet, hard flesh					Baking
Jonagold	Sweet, aromatic, juicy, crisp	Fresh		Sauce		
Jonamac	Similar to McIntosh but better flavor and firmness	Fresh				
Liberty	Sweetly sub-acid, crisp, fine-textured; best for pie!	Fresh			**Pie!**	
Lodi	Sour, grainy, poor keeper; magic as sauce!			**Sauce!**	Pie	
Macoun	Delicately aromatic, tart, crisp, juicy, spicy	Fresh				
McIntosh	Tart, semi-firm	Fresh	Salad			
Northern Spy	Tangy, robust, juicy, keeps very well; pies!	Fresh			**Pie!**	Baking
Paulared	Mildly tart, creamy, firm			Sauce	Pie	
Red Delicious	Very sweet, becomes dull in storage					
Transparent	Very early, very sour, won't store; sauce king!			**Sauce!**	Pie	
Winesap	Very juicy, winey sweet-sour flavor				Pie	Baking

Adapted from Cornell University Dept. of Fruit and Vegetable Sciences ratings, Ithaca, NY.

Tangy Green Applesauce

If you are ready for something completely different from commercial applesauce (sweet, bland, mealy, cinnamon-blotted . . . why do we eat it?!), here is a simple recipe for something vastly more interesting. We think of it as the Riesling of applesauce.

You'll have to search out one of a couple of apple varieties that are somewhat unusual, but once you've got them, the preparation is a snap. And the result is a creamy, piquant purée—light green in color and more liquid than you're used to—that will quench you and stimulate your palate like no applesauce you've had before. You can make large batches during the very limited season when the crucial apple varieties are available, freeze servings in multiple plastic containers, and defrost them throughout the year. These apple varieties are not for eating out of hand—they are terrible unprocessed! They also do not keep longer than a few days after picking (they literally turn to mush), so plan to process them immediately.

Lodi or Transparent apples
Sugar

Find a local supplier of Lodi apples (developed in the Finger Lakes in the 1920s, but available from quality producers around the United States). Lodis are one of the very first varieties to ripen, so start looking in July (or earlier, depending on the part of the country you live in). If you can't find Lodis, use Transparents (an even older heirloom early apple that has similar qualities). These heirloom varieties are worth a hunt. (See Resources for a great Web tool that locates orchards growing a particular apple variety.)

If you own a large French food mill, simply quarter the apples whole, add a very small amount of water, and boil until the flesh is soft. Then run the mash through the mill. French food mills are relatively inexpensive and easy to use, and by allowing you to keep the skins on the apples during cooking they enhance both vitamin content and flavor.

Alternatively, you can purée the cooked apples in a food processor. In this case, you must core and peel them before cooking.

Add sugar to taste. These are very tart apples, so it may take a bit—think rhubarb—but don't overdo it; enjoy a bit of pucker. And never add cinnamon or other spices that would compete with the Riesling-like zing of these apples. Always serve icy cold.

This sauce freezes beautifully; sometimes we think freezing even enhances its unusual creamy consistency.

Morning Glory Salad

Before you scan the ingredient list, wrinkle your nose, and flip to the next page, give this a chance! Yes, the combination of ingredients is unusual, and it looks like it might be über-healthy and therefore not appetizing. But it's a tasty mix, and the ingredient that we initially thought was the strangest (banana) is the flavor key. If you can use local apples and honey, all the better.

1 small head lettuce (iceberg or other), shredded
2 bananas, sliced
¾ cup raisins
¾ cup walnuts, chopped
1 large apple, chopped
3 ounces orange juice concentrate, undiluted
½ cup olive oil
2 Tablespoons honey
2 Tablespoons apple-cider vinegar
1 teaspoon poppy seeds

Combine the first five items. Whisk the rest of the ingredients into a vinaigrette. Make sure the honey is quite liquified (may require warming) before adding cold orange juice concentrate, or it will harden and refuse to combine with the other ingredients. Dress the salad.

Serves 8–10.

Adapted from a recipe by the Junior League of Rochester, NY.

24-Hour Cranberry Salad

This and the next dish, Whisker Salad, are old-fashioned family recipes. Since cranberries are in season only in the fall (and hard to find any other time of year), this treat has become an indelible part of our family's Thanksgiving and Christmas dinners. It tastes like nothing else we've ever eaten—and is beautiful to look at, too! (Anti-marshmallow militants are free to bounce right over these two recipes.)

> 1 12-ounce package of fresh cranberries
> 5–6 ounces of mini marshmallows
> ½ cup sugar
> ½ cup apple, chopped
> ½ cup walnuts, chopped
> 1 large can pineapple chunks, drained
> 1 cup heavy cream

Pulse the cranberries in a food processor until they are in pea-sized chunks. In a mixing bowl, stir cranberries together with the marshmallows and sugar, and chill overnight. (Thus the "24-Hours.")

The next day, add the apples, nuts, and pineapple chunks and mix gently. In a small bowl, whip the heavy cream with an electric beater until peaks form, then carefully fold the whipped cream into the other ingredients.

Serves 8–10.

Whisker Salad

Whereas the previous recipe features crimson cranberries, this one sparkles with mandarin oranges and coconut (the ingredient that gives the salad its name). This is comfort food at its finest, but the tropical fruit makes it light enough for summertime fare.

2 small cans mandarin oranges, drained
2 cups mini marshmallows
2 cups sweetened coconut
1 large can crushed pineapple, drained
1 16 oz. container sour cream

Mix the first four ingredients in a large bowl, fold in the sour cream, and serve. It can be eaten at room temperature or chilled.

Serves 8–10.

Pear & Gorgonzola Salad

The interesting thing about this salad is the bitterness of the vegetables in contrast with the sweetness of the pears and the candied walnuts. This is the kind of salad you can have fun with through different added ingredients and variations of the dressing. Make the candied walnuts first.

Candied Walnuts

> 1 egg white, whipped until thick
> 3 Tablespoons sugar
> 1 cup walnuts

Mix sugar and nuts into the whipped egg white. Line a baking sheet with parchment paper, pour mixture into pan, and bake at 350 degrees for 15 to 20 minutes, stirring occasionally. Allow to cool completely before handling.

Next assemble the salad.

> 1 ripe pear, sliced
> ½ cup radicchio, chopped fine
> ½ cup Belgian endive, chopped fine
> A handful of fresh mixed greens
> A sprinkling of Gorgonzola cheese
> A handful of candied walnuts
> Olive oil and balsamic vinegar to taste

Place all ingredients in a salad bowl, then dress with olive oil and balsamic vinegar to taste. Serve with some extra Gorgonzola on top.

Serves 4.

Adapted from a recipe by Cobblestone Restaurant in Geneva, NY.

Reinventing Yogurt

Upstate New York has long been one of the leading milk-producing regions in America, and in recent years area farmers and their cows have been increasing annual milk output by 10 to 12 percent every year. Despite that rapid expansion, the region is today approaching the point of requiring even more milk than the state's many farmers and rolling green hills can produce. The reason: some highly imaginative innovation in the production of new dairy products sold across the nation.

New York is now the top U.S. producer of sour cream, cottage cheese, and other specialized dairy foods, and yogurt production—one of today's hottest food segments—is growing in leaps and bounds. Two local companies—Chobani and Fage—recently helped turn so-called Greek yogurts into a booming national grocery category. Greek yogurt is zingier, higher in protein, and much thicker than mass-market yogurt because liquid is strained out of the milk before it is cultured.

An even more unusual new product now being made in the Finger Lakes is a line of vegetable yogurts from a company called aMaMa. Manufactured in Romulus near Seneca Lake, with some technical help from Cornell University, the lineup includes carrot, butternut squash, beet, sweet potato, and other flavors—even a spicy yogurt flavored with curry, turmeric, hot peppers, and garlic, inspired by the founder's East Indian heritage. Though savory yogurts were unheard of in America until recently, the new products (marketed as Vege'Yo' and SpicyYo') are getting rave reviews from grocery-product gurus.

Greek yogurts and vegetable yogurts work great in cooking as well. Try them in place of plain yogurt in the following recipes: Apple Yogurt Salad, page 117; Chocolate Sauerkraut Cake, page 183; and Pear Bread, page 26.

Tahini-Yogurt Lemon Dressing & Dipping Sauce

½ cup tahini

½ cup Greek yogurt

½ cup water (or more if you prefer thinner consistency)

3 Tablespoons grape-seed or olive oil

Juice of 1 large or 2 small lemons

1 clove garlic, chopped fine

¼ teaspoon ground cumin

¼ teaspoon paprika

½ teaspoon salt

Fresh (or dried) basil and dill to taste

Place all ingredients in a blender and purée until smooth. Dressing can be refrigerated for a week.

Makes approximately 1½ cups.

High-End Hydroponics

Cornell University, in the heart of the Finger Lakes, runs a special program in Controlled Environment Agriculture where researchers investigate new ways of producing food—like hydroponics, where plants are grown in nutrient-rich water rather than in soil. In the late 1990s, the university and private-sector partners built a large greenhouse to test methods for producing lettuce hydroponically year-round in snowy Upstate New York.

Today, the operation has been spun off to a local organization that employs disabled persons for the labor-intensive jobs of hand-seeding, transplanting, and packaging the grown plants. The seedlings float in channels of water about a foot deep, in which nutrients, oxygen, temperature, and other variables are computer controlled. Lighting is carefully timed to maximize growth. The plants think they are in Hawaii.

And after about one month afloat, they have developed from tiny seeds to lush heads of delicious lettuce (Boston, Romaine), greens (arugula, bok choy, mixed), or basil. The current operation yields about 10,000 perfect, consistent heads every week, and the operators are now planning additional greenhouses. Sold in supermarkets under the Finger Lakes Fresh brand, these intensely crisp, super-fresh greens are snatched up by consumers across New York and six other states—from Vermont to Maryland.

A different local entity is growing tomatoes indoors hydroponically. This source of year-round fresh vegetables in cool-weather New York has likewise proven wildly popular.

Other systems for growing high-quality food plants without soil are starting up nearby. Morrisville agricultural college and a central New York engineering firm have developed a greenhouse where the waterborne nutrients for the hydroponic greens come not from fertilizer but from the sterilized waste of tilapia fish farmed in tanks on the premises. (The fish will also be harvested for consumers.) A commercial operation employing this method to grow lettuce, greens, basil, and soon tomatoes (with the help of 8,000 fish) opened in the hamlet of Sherrill in 2011.

As lessons are learned and the energy, labor, and overall economic efficiencies of these operations increase, it is estimated that Controlled Environment Agriculture may become a half-billion-dollar industry for Upstate New York within the decade. And if it can succeed in the wintry Finger Lakes, then year-round production of beautiful local produce is within the reach of many other areas of the United States as well.

Arugula Salad
with Pecans & Pomegranate

Interplay between the bitter arugula and the candied pecans and fruity dressing makes for an interesting side dish or starter salad. The pomegranate seeds could easily be replaced by a fresh or dried fruit of your choice if you cannot find pomegranate seeds (although do try—they're scrumptious!).

Large bunch of fresh arugula
Seeds from a fresh pomegranate
    (or one package of pomegranate seeds)
2 small shallots, peeled and thinly sliced
1 cup candied pecans (purchase or make
    following the recipe below)
Orange vinaigrette (recipe follows)

Toss all ingredients together and serve on chilled plates as a starter or after the meal.

If you've never worked with fresh pomegranate before, quarter the fruit and, working over a bowl, use your fingers to separate the seeds from the skin and membrane. (Be careful of clothing—the juice stains.) If you're having trouble separating the seeds from little bits of membrane, add water to the bowl. The membrane pieces will float to the top where you can skim them off, then drain and the seeds are ready for use.

Candied Pecans

1 egg white, whipped until thick
2 Tablespoons brown sugar
2 Tablespoons white sugar
½ Tablespoon cinnamon
½ teaspoon nutmeg
Pinch of salt
1 cup pecan halves

Mix all ingredients into the whipped egg white. Line a baking sheet with parchment paper, pour mixture into pan, and bake at 350 degrees for 15 to 20

minutes, stirring occasionally. Allow to cool completely before handling.

Orange Vinaigrette

> 1 orange, zested and juiced
> 2 Tablespoons apple-cider vinegar
> 2 Tablespoons sugar
> 1½ teaspoons Dijon mustard
> ½ cup olive oil
> Salt and pepper to taste

Mix juice, zest, vinegar, sugar, and mustard together with a whisk. Slowly add oil. Season to taste with salt and freshly ground black pepper. Toss into salad with nuts and other ingredients.

Adapted from a recipe by Hazelnut Kitchen in Trumansburg, NY.

Super Sprouts

Another rising Finger Lakes business—a kind of kissing cousin to the hydroponics industry described in High-End Hydroponics (page 127)—is the production of edible sprouts. Springwater Sprouts, for instance, is a family-run firm in Honeoye Falls, New York, that produces more than 50 vegetable products for local groceries. Every year, they supply the region with more than half-a-million pounds of crunchy sprouts (from alfalfa, bean, onion, radish, broccoli, and other seeds) for salads and cooking.

Their broccoli sprouts are a particularly amazing product. Scientists have long known that broccoli, cauliflower, cabbage, kale, and other "cruciferous" vegetables contain chemicals that lower the risk of cancer. These compounds are especially concentrated when the plants first sprout.

Researchers at the Johns Hopkins School of Medicine found that the concentration of protective chemicals in broccoli sprouts is 20 to 50 times what it is in full-grown broccoli plants. Thus, a little more than an ounce of broccoli sprouts provides enough daily antioxidant compounds to cut the risk of colon cancer in half. One would have to eat two pounds of mature broccoli a day to get the same benefit.

The Johns Hopkins researchers developed a broccoli strain that is especially high in anticancer compounds, and tender and pungent as a sprout; these patented sprouts are now grown not only by Springwater but also by ten other growers around the country. Go to broccosprouts.com to search your area.

Greens Salad with Sprouts, Grapes & Pecans

4 Tablespoons pecan pieces, crushed
3 cups broccoli (or other) sprouts
4 cups mixed baby salad greens (or baby spinach)
1 cup seedless grapes, halved
Salt and pepper to taste
Raspberry vinaigrette or other favorite dressing

In large bowl, mix all ingredients together and toss well.
Serves 4.

Turkey & Sprout Roll-Ups

1 cup mayonnaise
6–8 Tablespoons picante sauce
2 teaspoons chili powder
1 Tablespoon cumin
12 small soft tortillas
24 thin deli slices of turkey breast
10 cups broccoli (or other) sprouts
Salt and pepper to taste

Combine mayonnaise, picante sauce, chili powder, and cumin. Spread one tablespoon of this mixture on tortilla and top with turkey and sprouts. Roll, and chill before serving.
Makes 12 roll-ups.

Greek Sprout Salad

2 cups broccoli (or other) sprouts
1 cup mushrooms, sliced
1 cup green pepper, chopped
4 cups Romaine lettuce, shredded
½ cup feta cheese
1 cup black olives
2 tomatoes, cut up
1 cucumber, cut up
Salt and pepper to taste
Light oil and vinegar dressing

In large bowl, mix ingredients together and toss well.
Serves 4.

Spinach & Strawberry Salad

Lovely to look at and full of surprises for your mouth, this dish is summery and good for you. Any soft sheep's cheese will do—experiment with local cheeses and find your favorite. The main goal with the cheese is to balance out the sweet and sour dressing, which has an unexpected mix of flavors and a nice crunch from the seeds.

⅛ cup balsamic vinegar

¼ cup honey

1 Tablespoon sesame seeds

½ teaspoon poppy seeds

1 teaspoon onion, finely minced

⅛ teaspoon Worcestershire sauce

⅛ teaspoon paprika

¼ cup olive oil

4 cups fresh spinach, preferably baby spinach

1 cup, or more, halved fresh strawberries

¼ to ½ cup feta cheese or any sheep's milk cheese

Freshly ground black pepper to taste

First make the dressing. Combine the honey and vinegar, then add the seeds, onion, Worcestershire sauce, paprika, and oil, and stir or shake until well mixed.

Arrange the spinach, strawberries, and cheese in a serving dish and generously season with freshly ground black pepper. Dress to taste, and store any leftover dressing in the fridge for future use.

Serves 4–6.

Maple & Balsamic Vinegar Salad Dressing

3 Tablespoons balsamic vinegar

2 Tablespoons maple syrup

1 Tablespoon lime juice

1 teaspoon dry mustard

1 rounded teaspoon cilantro, chopped

½ teaspoon salt

¼ teaspoon black pepper

1 clove garlic, minced

½ cup extra-virgin olive oil

Mix together all the ingredients except the oil, then whisk in oil until dressing is emulsified. Without being cloying, this has a distinctively maple flavor, so use on salads where a sweeter dressing is appropriate. Store excess in refrigerator.

Makes 1 cup.

Irish Muscle, Irish Stomachs

In *Erie Water,* Upstate New York novelist Walter Edmonds chronicles the heroic effort that went into hand digging New York's famous 363-mile canal and building its 83 stone locks. He provides vivid descriptions of the Irish laborers who accomplished the hardest tasks—like pawing through the muck of Montezuma swamp, and grubbing the deep channel through three and one-half miles of stone at Lockport:

> *Edwin Brown had cooked the breakfast for the new gang. In the main room he heard them stirring in their bunks. O'Mory, the boss, with his thick black beard stuffed inside his shirt to drink his tea, was asking for more bacon...*
> *These wild Irishers, who had chopped at stumps, who had shoveled where half of each shovelful ran back at their toes, who had wheeled barrows, who had had the sun on their backs, the frost in their feet, the cold wet against their bellies, the ague and fever in their lungs, who had had stumps to pull, and piles to drive in quicksand, limestone to blast, and rock to devil which no force but their own could loosen.*

In addition to those who dug New York's 13 canals, several million other Irish immigrants passed through the state. While not sticklers for cuisine, they left their mark on upstate culinary habits.

The signature comfort food of the Syracuse area, salt potatoes, is one Irish influence. The remains of an ancient sea left thick deposits of salt underneath much of central New York, and in the Syracuse area natural salt springs brought brine to the surface. Prior to the era of refrigeration, salt was valued highly for its use in preserving meats and other foods. So a large industry grew up in the region devoted to boiling the natural brine until nothing but crystalline salt was left, which was then shipped down the Erie Canal.

The workers tending the large boiling vats, many of them Irish, got in the habit of bringing a pocketful of small potatoes to work and dumping them into the boiling brine to make their lunch. Because of the high boiling point of water with lots of salt in it, these spuds come out creamy smooth, with a cracked salt-crunchy skin. You'll automatically get a side of these at the Dinosaur Bar-B-Que, at Baker's Chicken Shack at the New York State Fair, and at church suppers across the Finger Lakes. Local potatoes are often sold with a big container of salt included right in the bag.

Syracuse Salt Potatoes

Here is a basic recipe for this Upstate New York favorite.

> 8 cups water
> ¾ cup salt
> 3 pounds well-scrubbed small potatoes
>   (plum size is ideal), with skins left on
> ½ stick butter, melted
> Pepper or herbs of your choice

Bring the salt and water to a boil, add potatoes. Cook about 25 minutes, or until just tender (don't overcook to mushiness). Drain, add butter, and toss potatoes to coat. Add pepper or herbs to taste.

Serves 5–6.

Roasted Root Vegetables

This dish is aromatic and warming, great for a winter's evening. Made from vegetables you can keep around for months without spoilage, it is unfussy, inexpensive, and wholesome—yet elegantly tasty. You can substitute other root vegetables for slight variations of flavor or color.

1 cup rutabaga, peeled and diced into half-inch pieces
1 cup parsnips, peeled and sliced one quarter-inch thick
1 cup turnips, peeled and sliced one quarter-inch thick
¼ cup shallots, green onions, or leeks, sliced
3 garlic cloves, chopped
¼ cup squash-seed or olive oil
1 teaspoon salt
½ teaspoon freshly ground black pepper
½ teaspoon dried basil
½ teaspoon dried thyme
½ teaspoon dried oregano
2 Tablespoons fresh parsley, chopped

In an oven-proof dish with a cover, toss all the ingredients except the parsley and then bake covered for one and one-half hours at 375 degrees. The vegetables will caramelize slightly when they are done. Toss with parsley and serve.

Serves 4–6.

Adapted from a recipe by Simply Red Bistro in Ovid, NY.

Maple-Glazed Carrots

2 Tablespoons olive oil
1–2 shallots, sliced
1 pound carrots, sliced thinly on a diagonal
Salt and pepper to taste
Sprinkle of fresh (or dried) thyme
2–3 Tablespoons maple syrup

Heat olive oil in a skillet at medium-low. Add shallots and carrots, and salt and pepper to taste. Sauté for about 10 minutes. Add thyme and maple syrup. Turn heat up to medium. Stir occasionally and simmer for about 15 more minutes, until the shallots and carrots begin to caramelize.

Serves 4–6.

Courtesy of Ithaca Farmer's Market in Ithaca, NY.

Brussels Sprouts Confetti

For those of you who say "I don't like brussels sprouts," this concoction is for you. The sprouts are shredded thinly, much as cabbage is for cole slaw, and infused with simple but satisfying flavors.

> 2 Tablespoons squash-seed or other oil
> ¼ cup shallots, sliced
> 1½ pound brussels sprouts, shredded by slicing thinly
> Salt and pepper to taste
> 1½ cups chicken stock
> 2 Tablespoons butter

Heat the oil in a sauté pan and add the shallots. Once they are becoming translucent, add the shredded brussels sprouts, salt, and pepper. Sauté for about a minute. Add the chicken stock and allow to cook until the brussels sprouts are bright green.

Remove from heat, add butter and toss until it is melted. If desired, add additional salt and freshly ground pepper.

Serves 8.

Adapted from a recipe by Next Door Bar & Grill in Pittsford, NY.

Yam Soufflé

You mightn't think an earthy vegetable like a yam could ever take on a fluffy and refined flavor, but that's exactly the transformation that takes place in this sweet dish. This is a beloved feature of our Thanksgiving and other holiday meals, but can be enjoyed year-round. It's different from any other sweet-potato/yam-based concoction we've run into over the years. The nuts and the tropical extracts are what set the taste apart, and the light consistency is a signature.

4 pounds (3–4 tubers) yams or sweet potatoes
½ cup butter
1 cup sugar
4 large eggs
3 Tablespoons all-purpose flour
⅓ teaspoon baking powder
1 cup milk
¼ teaspoon salt
1 teaspoon vanilla extract
1 teaspoon almond extract
1 teaspoon coconut extract
½ cup pecans, chopped
4–6 Tablespoons brown sugar
¼ teaspoon cinnamon

Preheat oven to 350 degrees.

Peel yams and boil until soft, drain, then beat with an electric beater until smooth. Add the butter, sugar, eggs, flour, baking powder, milk, salt, and extracts. Whip with the beater until fluffy. Place in 9" x 13" glass, pottery, or metal baking pan.

In a small bowl, make a topping by mixing the pecans, brown sugar, and cinnamon. Sprinkle all of the topping over the yams and bake for one hour.

Serves 8.

Gruyère Grits Soufflé

A powerhouse of cheesy flavor and stick-to-your-ribs heartiness. Delicious right out of the oven, with a chewy brown crust on top. It also warms up beautifully. (We confess we sometimes even munch it cold.) For a wholly different experience, warm up servings with a dollop of salsa on top.

1 quart milk
1 stick butter
1 teaspoon salt
1 cup grits (regular, not instant)
6 ounces Gruyère cheese, grated
1 tomato, diced small
1 cup Parmesan cheese, grated

Heat milk, butter, and salt in a saucepan until butter is melted. Add grits and cook covered, stirring occasionally, for 10 to 15 minutes.

Turn oven on to 325 degrees.

Remove saucepan from heat and fold in grated Gruyère cheese. Let sit until melted. Beat until the grits and cheese are thoroughly combined. Then add diced tomato and lightly fold in.

Pour the mixture into an oven-safe dish. Top with the Parmesan cheese and bake uncovered for 30 minutes.

Serves 10.

Zucchini & Cannellini

We've included this among our side dishes, but with its beans, a mix of vegetables, and lots of cheese, this could easily be served as an entrée. It's very flavorful, and filling. You may want to serve in bowls rather than on a plate.

3 Tablespoons squash-seed or olive oil
3 smallish zucchinis, cut into small chunks
1 onion, chopped
2 teaspoons garlic, minced
1 large tomato, chopped
½ teaspoon dried thyme (or ½ Tablespoon fresh)
4–10 basil leaves, chopped
½ teaspoon salt
¼ teaspoon black pepper
1 can cannellini beans, drained and rinsed
¾ cup Parmesan cheese

Heat the oil and sauté zucchini, onion, and garlic for 5 to 10 minutes.

Stir in tomato, thyme, basil, salt, pepper, and beans. Cover and simmer 5 to 10 minutes, until zucchini is tender.

Stir in cheese, then add additional salt and pepper if desired.

Serves 6–8.

Quinoa with Almond & Apple

If you want to make this your main course, you can. The recipe has protein (quinoa), fresh fruit (apples), healthy fat (almonds), and it is just bursting with flavor due to the interesting spicing. It is also great as a side to grilled fish with Tomato & Peach Sauce for Fish (see page 74). Or simply pair it with a vegetable and a hunk of crusty bread.

1 cup quinoa, uncooked
Pinch of salt
1½ cups water
2 Tablespoons olive oil
1 clove garlic, diced
¼ of a large onion (or one small onion), diced
⅛ teaspoon cinnamon
¼ teaspoon ground cumin
½ teaspoon ground coriander
¼ teaspoon paprika
¼ teaspoon salt
¼ cup slivered almonds
½ apple, peeled, cored, and diced

Add the quinoa and salt to water and bring to a boil, turn down heat and simmer, covered, for 15 minutes or until the water has been absorbed.

Meanwhile, in a large skillet heat the olive oil and sauté the garlic and onion until they begin to caramelize slightly. Stir in the spices to make a paste, then add the almonds and apple and heat (do not cook).

Stir the cooked quinoa and the rest of the ingredients together and mix thoroughly. Serve warm.

Serves 4–6.

Adapted from a recipe by Stonecat Cafe in Hector, NY.

Lemony Kasha

Cooked kasha, or buckwheat kernels, have an earthy, nutty flavor. (See a description of buckwheat's deep and unusual central New York food history on page 38.) This dish is not for everyone, but if you enjoy buckwheat, use this as an alternative to rice or other starch, perhaps as a bed for meats and sauces.

2 Tablespoons butter, divided
1 onion, chopped
½ cup chopped green pepper
2 cups chicken broth
Zest of 1 lemon
Juice of 1 lemon
½ teaspoon salt
¼ teaspoon pepper
¾ cup kasha, uncooked

Melt half the butter in a skillet and lightly sauté onion and pepper. Add all other ingredients except kasha and bring to a boil.

In a separate medium-size saucepan with a cover, melt the rest of the butter and then dump kasha kernels into hot pan. Stir kasha over high heat until it is slightly toasted—about 2 to 3 minutes. Then carefully pour liquid into pan, cover, and simmer on very low heat until liquid is absorbed and kernels are tender—about 15 minutes.

Serves 6–8.

Zucchini Herb Casserole

This is a snap to make and can be endlessly modified depending on your tastes and what you have around. You may use any fresh herbs and other cheeses. Tomatoes are a delightful addition if you have good ripe ones available.

1 Tablespoon squash-seed or olive oil
3 to 4 medium zucchini or yellow squash, sliced
1 onion, chopped
Salt and pepper to taste
Light sprinkle of fennel seeds
6–10 fresh basil leaves
1 Tablespoon butter
¼ cup sour cream
¾ cup cheddar cheese, shredded
2 Tablespoons chives, chopped

Slowly sauté the zucchini and onion in olive oil, with salt and pepper. When the squash is just becoming tender, not mushy, layer it in the bottom of an oven-proof baking dish. Sprinkle with a few fennel seeds and layer on the basil, then set aside.

In a saucepan, melt the butter over low heat and then add the sour cream, cheese, and chives. Once the cheese is melted, drizzle over the zucchini. Bake at 350 degrees for 20 to 25 minutes.

Serves 4–6.

Maple Corn Pudding

Sometimes the Finger Lakes Iroquois made corn puddings sweetened with maple syrup, and this recipe pays homage to those flavors. But don't be mistaken—this is a savory side dish, only slightly sweet (think of the sweetness of corn bread). It is easy in the summer when fresh corn is available, but thawed frozen corn can be substituted without a problem.

1 stick butter
2 eggs, beaten
2 teaspoons salt
Freshly ground black pepper to taste
2 Tablespoons maple syrup
2 cups milk
⅞ cup flour
2 cups corn kernels (cut off the cob
    or defrosted frozen corn)
¼ cup red bell pepper, diced

Place butter in a baking pan (about 10" x 13") and melt in oven as it preheats to 350 degrees. In a bowl, whisk together the eggs, salt, black pepper, maple syrup, milk, and flour. When smooth, fold in the corn and diced red pepper.

Remove baking pan from oven as soon as butter is melted. Pour liquid butter into corn mixture, stir well, then return all to the baking pan. Bake in oven for about an hour, or until the pudding is golden brown on top and firm in the center (test with fork or toothpick).

Serves approximately 8.

Fresh Eggs on the Way

America is in the midst of a backyard-chicken boom. Not only in the country but even in towns, tens of thousands of Americans are now keeping chickens for their eggs (as myriad families, urban and non-urban, have for centuries). Given a few common sense rules—no roosters, limited numbers, adequate caging, sanitation guidelines—"chickens can peacefully and unobtrusively co-exist with people even in an urban environment," concludes Maine state veterinarian Donald Hoenig.

Among the major cities that now allow families to keep chickens in their backyards, garages, or roof decks: New York City, Brooklyn, Buffalo, Binghamton, Seattle, Houston, Los Angeles, San Diego, Baltimore, Minneapolis, and scores of others. Hens and vegetable gardens go together beautifully as part of the movement toward more local, decentralized, natural, and traditional family living. There's something about henkeeping that can excite everyone from old-fashioned agrarians to neo-hippies to parents of young children. *Backyard Poultry* magazine is a good place to get an overview of today's big interest in small flocks.

Fresh eggs are much tastier than ones that have been in transit for a while. We feed our hens flax seed, purchased from a local Amish farmer, which makes the eggs high in cholesterol-lowering omega-3—an extremely healthy fatty acid that many of us are deficient in. It is also found in nuts, seeds, and oily fish. You too can create a backyard superfood in this way, while enjoying free comedy performances. (Chickens are a blast to watch.) Or buy fresh local eggs from a neighbor who keeps hens.

And if you live in some grinchy town that forbids small-scale chicken keeping by responsible families (our home village of Cazenovia, New York, recently banned the birds amidst much clucking and sarcasm from one or two politicians), fight back! Chickens are much healthier, safer, and less obtrusive than pet dogs—which is why more and more localities are allowing families to keep chickens for eggs, without problems or controversy. Our Resources section lists articles sketching the depth, breadth, and overall health of today's rising interest in backyard chickens.

Sweets

Happiness makes up in height

for what it lacks in length.

—poem by Robert Frost

Little Ricotta Cheesecakes

Before you think "this sounds too fussy for me," take a second look. This is probably the easiest cheesecake recipe out there, and also one of the most satisfying. It is surprisingly delicate, and can be presented elegantly.

16 ounces cream cheese (2 packages),
    at room temperature
4 ounces ricotta cheese
¾ cup sugar
3 eggs
2 extra egg yolks
1 teaspoon vanilla extract
5 Tablespoons heavy cream
Paper cupcake liners
Lemon Curd (see recipe on page 151)
Berries

Preheat oven to 300 degrees.

In a large bowl, mix cheeses and sugar together with an electric beater until smooth. In a small bowl, combine eggs, yolks, and vanilla. Then gradually add the eggs to the cheese mixture. Add heavy cream and mix well.

Line a 12-well muffin or cupcake pan with the paper liners. Pour or carefully spoon the batter into each well, being careful not to overfill (stop just below the top of the liner). Set the muffin pan in a larger pan or a cookie sheet with sides and add about a half-inch or so of water. Bake for about one hour.

Remove cupcake pan from oven and let cakes cool in the pan for a few minutes, then transfer the cheesecakes with the paper still on to a cooling rack. When they are no longer hot, chill them in the refrigerator for 1 to 2 hours.

When you are ready to serve them, place each cheesecake upside down on a small plate, then carefully peel away the paper. Serve with a dollop of Lemon Curd. Add a few fresh berries.

Makes about 12 mini cheesecakes.

Adapted from a recipe by Hazelnut Kitchen in Trumansburg, NY.

Lemon Pound Cake with Lemon Curd

This is a light, moist pound cake, perfect with a pot of hot tea. The curd is a beautiful complement—tart and zesty. With a scattering of fresh fruit on top it makes for a colorful and flavor-packed dessert.

1½ cups flour
1½ teaspoons baking powder
A pinch of salt
1½ sticks butter, softened
1¾ cups white sugar
3 eggs
½ cup buttermilk
Zest of 1 lemon
3 Tablespoons fresh lemon juice

Preheat oven to 325 degrees. Butter and flour a loaf pan approximately 9" x 5" x 3".

Whisk flour, baking powder, and salt together. Using a mixer, beat in the butter, and all but a couple tablespoons of the sugar (which you should hold back).

When all is well blended, beat in the eggs one at a time. Finally add the buttermilk, lemon zest, and lemon juice, and mix.

Pour batter into the loaf pan and sprinkle the remaining sugar on top. Bake for 45 to 55 minutes. (Test for doneness by inserting a wooden toothpick or fork into the center of the cake; it should come out clean with no batter clinging to it.)

While the cake is baking, prepare the lemon curd.

Lemon Curd

⅓ cup fresh lemon juice

2 eggs

¾ cup white sugar

¾ stick butter

Place the lemon juice, eggs, and sugar in a heavy-bottom pot on medium heat, and whisk until the mixture is thick and bubbling. Whisk in the butter.

Remove from heat and allow to cool. Place a piece of plastic wrap directly on the curd as it cools, so that no skin forms on top. You may refrigerate if necessary until ready to use.

To serve, cut the pound cake into fairly thin slices, top with lemon curd and fresh whipped cream. In season, add blueberries, blackberries, strawberries, sliced peaches, or raspberries on top.

Serves 8–10.

Adapted from a recipe by Simply Red Bistro in Ovid, NY.

Blueberry Heaven

U-pick fruit and vegetable farms are a great American tradition. Upstate New York is richer with them than any part of the country: a local website lists 135 different U-pick operations in the Finger Lakes region, offering visitors the chance to harvest for themselves everything from pears, gooseberries, and green beans to sour cherries, peas, and fresh flowers. One place frequented by our family grows 60 different varieties of apples. To find a U-pick farm in your part of the United States, start at pickyourown.org.

Blueberries are one of the easiest fruits to pick yourself. They can of course be served without any peeling, pitting, or preparation. And they freeze beautifully.

We sometimes pick 30 pounds at a time, stow them in our freezer, then pull them out in the dead of winter for pancakes or muffins. Our kids love to munch them frozen, one at a time. Sprinkle the frozen berries on granola or cereal with milk and they add a half-icy zing to breakfast. And, nutritionally, blueberries are one of the healthiest antioxidant foods available.

Being indigenous to the Finger Lakes (where the Iroquois used to pound them with dried meat to make pemmican), there are many wonderful blueberry patches to choose from. Grisamore is a family farm with fifth-generation owners living on-site, where the bushes stand like walls and produce marble-sized berries that can be raked into buckets while comfortably standing. At Glenhaven, run by a Cornell College of Agriculture and Life Sciences grad, 11 acres of bushes provide fruit not only for fresh picking but also for the blueberry wines made on-site. Our sentimental favorite, Luce Farm, sits high on a ridge between Seneca and Cayuga lakes, overlooking the water. Lots of Mennonite women in bonnets and long dresses come to pick at this peaceful spot where the only sounds are rustling wind and birdsong and the hum of corn dryers in the late summer.

There's an old aphorism that firewood warms you twice—once when you cut it, a second time when you burn the logs. Similarly, berry picking can fill your eyes, stomach, and soul once when you harvest, and then again later when you consume.

Blueberry Egg-White Cake

This is served at Maxie's Supper Club as a multi-layer cake with a lemon filling, but in our test kitchen we found the blueberry cake to be sufficiently flavorful that we think home cooks will want to save steps and serve it by itself. If you'd like to add your own vanilla, buttercream, or lemon frosting (as we did in the picture), feel free to experiment.

3 egg whites
2⅛ cups all-purpose flour
1⅛ cups sugar
2 teaspoons baking powder
1 teaspoon salt
1 stick butter, softened
1 cup heavy cream
1 teaspoon vanilla extract
½ pint to 1 pint fresh blueberries
Powdered sugar
Whipped cream

Preheat oven to 350 degrees. Butter and flour a 9" x 13" pan (or two smaller layer-cake pans) and set aside.

Beat egg whites until soft peaks form (about 2 minutes), then refrigerate. Whisk together flour, sugar, baking powder, and salt. Using an electric mixer, add in butter, cream, and vanilla. Beat on high speed until very smooth, about 2 minutes.

Hand fold in the beaten egg whites until fully incorporated, then fold in the blueberries. Pour batter into cake pan and bake for about 30 minutes, until toothpick or fork inserted in the center comes out clean. Dust the top with powdered sugar, then cool. Serve with whipped cream, and a few more berries for garnish.

Serves 8–10.

Adapted from a recipe by Maxie's Supper Club in Ithaca, NY.

Rustic Spice Apple Cake

There is a reason this is called "Spice Apple" cake and not "Apple Spice"—it is quite gingery and spice-infused. While the apples are important, they take the second seat in this concoction. It is best to use a soft cooking apple that will become mushy and almost melt into the cake. (See our apple chart on page 118 for ideas.)

This cake has a tension of flavors and textures: Underneath, it's rustic, even a little primitive (thanks to the molasses and the surprise ingredient of cornmeal). Up top, though, it's velvety rich (caramel and cream). This makes for a quirky and unexpected effect on your palate.

Don't be afraid to soak the cake in caramel and then slather it with cream—it needs all the elements together to work. Being such a hearty and rich dish, you won't want to cut the portions too large.

1 cup cornmeal
1 cup flour
1¼ Tablespoons cinnamon
1½ Tablespoons ground allspice
1½ Tablespoons ground ginger
1 Tablespoon ground cloves
1½ teaspoons salt
1½ teaspoons baking powder
1½ teaspoons baking soda
¼ cup white sugar
½ cup raisins
2 apples, cut into marble-size pieces, skin on
½ cup vegetable oil
1 egg
¼ cup blackstrap molasses
¼ cup dark rum
¼ cup maple syrup

Preheat oven to 375 degrees. In a large bowl, mix the dry ingredients together, then add the raisins and apples. Separately whisk together all the wet ingredients. Combine wet ingredients into dry ingredients. Place batter in a 9-inch square greased baking pan. Bake for 20 to 30 minutes. While baking, make the caramel sauce.

Caramel Sauce

        1 cup white sugar

        3 cups heavy cream (save one of the three for whipping)

        1 cinnamon stick

        ¼ cup apple cider

Place the sugar in a heavy-bottom pot on medium heat, and continuously stir with a wooden spoon (the sugar will slowly melt and caramelize once all the sugar has melted). Pour in two cups of heavy cream very slowly. (It will sputter and boil up a little; it may even clump, but have no fear.) Turn down the heat to low, and stir occasionally as the cream comes to temperature. Add in the cinnamon stick and apple cider and simmer for about 15 minutes (discard the cinnamon stick once fully simmered). Allow to cool slightly. (Store extra sauce in a sealed container. The caramel and the cider will separate slightly while being stored; just stir them together every time you use.)

Whip the remaining cup of cream.

To serve, slice the cake and place each serving in a bowl. Top with ¼ cup to ⅓ cup of caramel sauce, and then pile with whipped cream. Dust with a sprinkling of cinnamon.

Makes one 9-inch cake.

Adapted from a recipe by Simply Red Bistro in Ovid, NY.

Pfeffernüsse Cookies

These spicy, fruity, chewy treats, which improve in flavor as they age and mellow, are a wonderful cookie for any time of year. But we can't bite into one without thinking of Christmas. Come Yuletide, these are the cookies that take over our oven, as family members clamor for batch after batch throughout the season. They're known as a baked good that will keep in tins for a long time—though they never last long enough in our house to test that out. This recipe (pronounced "feffernus") comes from our German relatives.

1 cup butter
1½ cups sugar
3 eggs
2 cups dates, chopped
1 cup walnuts, chopped
1 cup raisins
½ teaspoon ground cloves
1 teaspoon cinnamon
1 teaspoon allspice
1 teaspoon baking soda
1¾ cups flour
Powdered sugar

Preheat oven to 350 degrees.

Cream the butter and sugar together, then add the eggs. Chop the dates, walnuts, and raisins in a food processor. Then stir together all the ingredients, except the powdered sugar.

Scoop the dough into small rounded balls and place on cookie sheets. Bake for 9 to 15 minutes.

Let cool, then roll the cookies in powdered sugar. Store in tins.

Makes approximately 25 cookies.

Carrot Cake

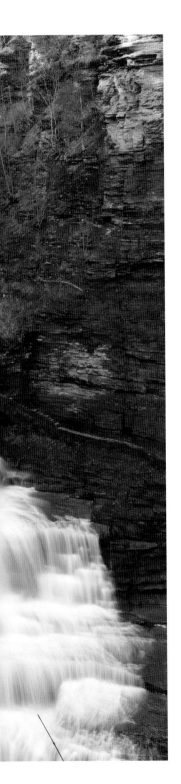

Okay, you can say it: This is one dessert that's good for me! It has 3 cups of carrots in it! Yes, it also has sugar and oil and the other staples of a good cake, but go ahead and convince yourself. This treat is worth it. We've eaten lots of carrot cakes but this one is much more natural, moist, and appealing than any runner-up we know. And the icing is the perfect match to the rest of the cake.

> 4 eggs
> 2 cups sugar
> 1¼ cups vegetable oil
> 2 cups sifted flour
> 2 teaspoons cinnamon
> 2 teaspoons baking soda
> 1 teaspoon salt
> 3 cups carrots, loosely grated
> 1 cup pecans or walnuts, chopped
> 1 teaspoon vanilla

Preheat oven to 350 degrees and butter and flour a 9" x 13" pan. Beat together the eggs and sugar until light, then slowly add the vegetable oil. Whisk together the flour, cinnamon, baking soda, and salt, and then add this to the wet ingredients. Stir in the carrots, nuts, and vanilla.

Pour the batter into the pan and bake for about 35 minutes. While it is baking, make the icing.

Icing

> 8 ounces cream cheese, at room temperature
> ½ cup butter, softened
> 2 cups powdered sugar
> 2 teaspoons vanilla

Cream together the cream cheese, butter, and powdered sugar. Stir in the vanilla, and spread over the cake after it has cooled. (You may use a spot of milk to thin the icing if it is too stiff.)

Makes one 9" x 13" cake.

Sun Sugar

Honey is the concentrated nectar of flowers—a form of stored solar energy. There are cave paintings showing that it has been collected and prized by humans for at least 8,000 years. Honey has interesting physical qualities—like its resistance to spoilage, which allows it to remain edible for decades or even centuries.

Honey contains many trace elements, including antioxidants and minerals. While mass-produced versions are blended and filtered into bland uniformity, local honey varies by the terrain, the local flora, and what was in bloom during the period while the bees gathered the nectar for that batch of honey.

If you allow your bees to make honey for a full season, and then harvest it once at the end of the year, the honey will be a mix of many flower nectars (spring orchards, summer trees, fall wildflowers, etc.). But by collecting at different times throughout the year, it is also possible to produce "monofloral" honey varieties that contain the nectar of primarily just one blossom. Add to this the differences in local weather, soil, and geology, and artisan honey becomes a varietal product similar to local varietal wines.

The fine Finger Lakes wine and food writer Michael Turback gives us some lovely images of the honey/wine parallel:

Each honey precisely reflects not only the flavor, color, and aroma of each floral source, but the characteristics of each year's growing season. Bright yellow locust honey typically draws mild, woody, grassy flavors from the large, fragrant blossoms of black locust trees. Basswood honey is suggestive of mint and green fruit with a pleasant bitterness on the finish. Honey from the alfalfa pasture has a subtle, soothing flavor and intoxicating honeysuckle aroma. Delicate white flowers of hard-to-find buckwheat grain yield an unmistakable mahogany-colored honey with a silky texture and nutty, robust character reminiscent of molasses.

Honey is not only an intrinsically valued ingredient in the food of the Finger Lakes; the field activity of honeybees is also essential to the production of many other signature foodstuffs from the region. Apples, sweet and sour cherries, raspberries, blackberries, blueberries, plums, pears, apricots, peaches, and melons are heavily dependent upon bees for the pollination that yields healthy fruit. Squash, cucumbers, pumpkins, many herbs, buckwheat, sunflowers, canola, soybeans, dairy clover, and alfalfa similarly produce better when bees are afield.

The collective amount of work done by bees, in their tiny daily micro-doses, is staggering. It takes two million flower visits and about 55,000 miles of flying (the equivalent of circling the earth more than twice) to gather enough nectar for a single pound of honey.

And that's not the end of the labor. The reason honey doesn't ferment and spoil like other sweet juices is because the bees continually remove water from it until it becomes a "supersaturated liquid" (containing more natural sugars than that amount of water can normally dissolve). They do this by fanning their wings over the open honeycomb cells—thousands of them working in shifts, 24/7—until the right amount of water has evaporated off.

In northern climates like the cool Finger Lakes, all this work of collecting and making the honey that will sustain the hive through the rest of the year (not to mention supplying humans who tap into the hive's stash) must be done in a period of only about 60 days. From mid-May to mid-July, while local flowers are at their peak, our bees must glean 12 months of life-giving energy from the fields and forests of central New York.

During a single warm June day, the bees in one hive may carry home several pounds of flower nectar. Considering that they must suck up this sugary liquid and then transport it using only their tiny bodies, often over long distances, this is quite a feat. Cornell University professor and local beekeeper Thomas Seeley calculates that "one foraging bee typically brings home a nectar load weighing about .001 ounces." Do the math on a hive that produces a hundred pounds of honey, and you'll agree: That delicious sticky treat on your granola or toast is—largely unobserved and unappreciated—a minor miracle.

Honey Spice Drops

A distinctive element of these cookies is the use of honey, which is not only delicious but a sweetener you can procure in your own locality. For the dipping sugar, be sure to use "organic cane sugar" if you can find it in your store. Not for some magical purity but for the texture—its grains are larger than plain granulated sugar, so it provides a nice crunch, as well as a beautiful clear shimmer on the top of these spicy cookies.

¼ cup honey
1 cup brown sugar
¾ cup shortening
1 egg
2¼ cups flour
1½ teaspoons baking soda
½ teaspoon salt
1 teaspoon ginger
½ teaspoon cinnamon
¼ teaspoon cloves
½ cup organic cane sugar (for dipping)

Combine the honey, brown sugar, shortening, and egg in a medium-size bowl and beat on low speed with a mixer until creamy.

In a separate bowl, mix the flour, baking soda, salt, and spices well. Then gradually beat the dry ingredients into the wet ingredients.

Shape the batter into balls, dip into the cane sugar, and flatten the balls into cookie patties using the bottom of a glass.

Bake the cookies at 350 degrees for 10 to 12 minutes.

Makes approximately 25 cookies.

Molasses Coconut Chews

These are homey, not fancy cookies. As the name implies, they are fairly dense, and the blackstrap molasses gives them a hearty flavor. This version is descended from an Old Sturbridge Village recipe.

1 cup white sugar
1 cup brown sugar
1 cup butter
2 eggs, beaten
2 teaspoons vanilla
¼ cup blackstrap molasses
4 cups flour
1½ teaspoons baking soda
1 teaspoon salt
1 cup shredded coconut

Preheat oven to 375 degrees.

Cream together the sugars with the butter. Add the eggs, vanilla, and molasses. Beat well.

In a separate bowl, combine the flour, baking soda, and salt. Once fully combined, add to the wet ingredients. Stir in the coconut, then shape the batter into balls.

Bake for 12 minutes. Don't overcook or they'll be dry.

Makes approximately 30 cookies.

Mohntorte

This is a traditional German cake that packs a rich earthy flavor and quite a crunch—thanks to the poppy seeds and almonds. Don't skip the whipped cream at the end, else you may find this cake a bit dry. We found it to be a delightful complement.

1 cup poppy seeds
1 cup almonds, finely chopped
1 cup bread crumbs
⅛ teaspoon ground cinnamon
⅛ teaspoon ground cloves
¼ teaspoon salt
1 teaspoon baking powder
1 cup butter, softened
1¼ cups powdered sugar
1 teaspoon grated lemon zest
1 teaspoon vanilla
1 teaspoon rum
9 eggs, separated into yolks and whites
1 cup plus 3 Tablespoons white sugar

Preheat oven to 350 degrees, and butter and flour a 9-inch bundt pan.

Mix poppy seeds, almonds, bread crumbs, cinnamon, cloves, salt, and baking powder, then set aside.

With a beater, cream the butter and powdered sugar, then add lemon zest, vanilla, and rum. Beat in one egg yolk at a time and then set aside.

In a separate bowl, whip the egg whites into soft peaks, gradually add sugar until stiff. Fold this by hand into the egg yolk mixture, being careful not to deflate the whites by stirring too vigorously. Then fold the poppy seed mixture into the wet ingredients.

Pour the batter into the pan and bake for 45 to 55 minutes.

Cool the cake for a few minutes in the pan, then turn it over onto a plate or platter. Cake will drop out of the pan as it cools.

While still slightly warm, dust with powdered sugar and serve with homemade whipped cream.

Makes one 9-inch bundt cake.

Adapted from a recipe by Dano's Heuriger in Lodi, NY.

Apple Brownies

These are a perfect, chewy treat when you are looking for good uses for fresh apples.

½ cup butter

⅞ cup sugar

1 egg

1 cup apples (any variety), chopped

1 cup walnuts, chopped

1 cup flour

½ teaspoon baking soda

½ teaspoon baking powder

½–1 teaspoon cinnamon

Preheat oven to 350 degrees.

Cream the butter and sugar together, then add the rest of the ingredients. Pour into a buttered and floured 9-inch square baking pan and bake for 30 to 40 minutes.

Makes 12 brownies.

Patsy's Molasses Cookies

This recipe comes from an old friend, a gifted baker who always had tantalizing smells wafting from her kitchen. Unlike some molasses cookies, these are thin, with a crunchy exterior and a soft, chewy middle. They are one of our all-time favorite sweets.

3/4 cup butter, softened
1 cup sugar
1 egg
1/4 cup molasses
2 cups flour
2 teaspoons baking soda
3/4 teaspoon ground cloves
1 teaspoon cinnamon
3/4 teaspoon ground ginger
Pinch of salt
Powdered sugar

Preheat oven to 325 degrees.

Cream together the butter and sugar. Add the egg and molasses.

In a separate bowl, combine the dry ingredients. Gradually add the dry ingredients into the wet and mix thoroughly. Bake on ungreased cookie sheets for about 7 minutes, or until just set. Let cool and roll in powdered sugar.

Makes approximately 25 cookies.

Pumpkin Bars

Fall wouldn't be fall without the occasional pumpkin-flavored baked good eaten with a cup of hot cider or tea, warming the body and soul against the increasingly chilly air. These are best sliced into skinny rectangles, so they can be picked up and eaten by hand.

> 2 cups sugar
> 4 eggs
> 1 cup vegetable oil
> 2 cups flour
> 1½ teaspoons baking powder
> 2 teaspoons cinnamon
> 1 teaspoon salt
> 1 teaspoon baking soda
> 1 cup canned pumpkin purée

Preheat oven to 325 degrees and grease an 11" x 18" jelly-roll pan with low sides.

Beat together the sugar and eggs, then add the oil. In a separate bowl, combine the dry ingredients. Then add the sugar, egg, and oil mixture to the flour mixture. Stir in the pumpkin.

Bake for 20 to 25 minutes. While the sheet is cooling, make the icing.

Icing

> 8 ounces cream cheese, at room
>   temperature
> ½ cup butter, softened
> 2 cups powdered sugar
> 2 teaspoons vanilla

Cream together the cream cheese and butter. Add powdered sugar. Stir in the vanilla. (You may use a spot of milk to thin the icing if it is too stiff.) Frost when bars are cool.

Makes one jelly-roll sheet.

Real Pie Crust

A light and flaky pie crust can be a little difficult to learn, and it helps if you have someone experienced to work alongside you the first few times. In our family, the techniques were passed over the years directly from mother, to daughter-in-law, to granddaughter. For those of you who don't have an in-person guide, we've tried to make the instructions below extra explicit. Just don't give up if it doesn't turn out well the first time! Making a good pie crust is an art that develops with experience, and once you've got it you can return to it again and again, like riding the proverbial bike. If you persevere you'll have a culinary skill for life.

1½ cups flour
A pinch of salt
½ cup shortening
⅓ cup cold water

In a small to medium-size bowl, combine the flour and salt. Cut the shortening into the mixture, using a pastry cutter. Do this until all of the shortening is the size of little peas, or smaller.

Add the cold water and quickly whisk the dough with a fork until it forms into a soft lump. Do not overmix.

Place the dough on a well-floured surface and split into two halves. Gently mold it into a round ball using your hands, and when it is well-formed, begin to roll it out with a floured rolling pin.

The key in rolling is not to press down too hard onto the dough. Simply roll it and allow it to take its time in stretching. Flip it often, dusting flour underneath to prevent it from sticking to the counter.

When the dough is about ⅛-inch thick, fold it over on itself, gently pick it up, and lay it across your pie pan. Unfold it and let it take the shape of the pan.

Place your filling inside, then repeat the process with the top crust.

Lay the top crust on the pie, cut around the dish to trim away any overhanging dough, then seal the top and bottom crust together by pinching them at the edges. (Leave an artful scalloped pattern if you can. In our family we can tell who made the pie by glancing at this detail!) Using fork tines, decoratively pierce a few vent holes into the top of the pie.

Bake the pie depending on the filling (see our Finger Lakes Apple Pie below).

Makes one 9-inch top-and-bottom-crust pie, or two 9-inch pies without tops.

Finger Lakes Apple Pie

This is a pristine classic. If you can find Liberty or Northern Spy apples, they are in a class by themselves for pie, and absolutely worth the effort. For other good alternatives, consult our chart of apple varieties on page 118. The apple you choose really matters.

You'll laugh to see how simple the filling below is, but that's its beauty—too many apple pies are gunked up with heavy spicing or cornstarch or too much sugar. Just follow the directions and you'll have a simple, flaky, fruity treat.

> 6–8 tart apples
> 1 Tablespoon flour
> 1 Tablespoon sugar
> ½–¾ cup sugar
> Several dabs of butter, total approx. 1 Tablespoon
> A light dusting of ground cinnamon

Preheat oven to 375 degrees.

Make pie crust (see our Real Pie Crust, on facing page). Do not pre-bake crust.

Peel and core apples. Sprinkle about a tablespoon each of flour and sugar on the bottom of the unbaked pie crust. Slice apples on top until the pie pan is filled with a layer of fruit about 2 inches deep.

Sprinkle the apples with ½ to ¾ cup of sugar (depending on the size of your pie, the tartness of your apples, and your preference in sweetness).

Place 4 to 5 dabs of butter on top. Sprinkle lightly with cinnamon.

Then lay the top crust over the fruit, pinch to seal together the edges of the top and bottom, and prick top a few times with a fork.

Place pie in oven. Remove after 45 minutes, or when top crust becomes nicely brown.

Makes one 9-inch pie.

Mojito Bars

Like lemon bars, these treats have a buttery melt-in-your-mouth crust that is baked first to prevent sogginess. On top is a limey, minty filling that boasts the same meld of flavors as the lime, mint, and rum drink known as a mojito. Like the drink, these are refreshing and crisp. Enjoy them as either a dessert or a snack.

Prep

   16 mint leaves, finely chopped
   4 Tablespoons of white rum

Combine mint and rum in a small bowl and set aside.

Crust

   1½ sticks soft butter
   ½ cup powdered sugar
   1¾ cup flour

Preheat oven to 350 degrees.

In a mixing bowl, use an electric beater to cream the butter and the sugar, then add the flour. Press mixture into the bottom of an ungreased 13" x 9" pan, or two round 9-inch pans. Bake for 5 to 10 minutes, until slightly golden brown.

Filling

   ¼ cup flour
   4 eggs
   1½ cups sugar
   ¼ teaspoon salt
   1 Tablespoon lime zest
   ⅔ cup lime juice
   2 Tablespoons heavy cream

Whisk together the filling ingredients, then add the rum/mint mixture and whisk again. Pour the filling into the baked crust and put back into the oven for 15 to 20 minutes. Cool, then dust with powdered sugar.

Serves 10–12.

Adapted from a recipe by Arad Evans Inn in Fayetteville, NY.

French Chocolate Pudding

This is a classic dessert that the gifted chef of La Petite Maison learned to make from his French grandmother, Hélène.

2 eggs
¾ cup sugar
1 Tablespoon cornstarch
2 cups milk
½ cup heavy cream
4 ounces dark semi-sweet chocolate
Whipped cream to decorate
Pepperidge Farm Pirouette cookies

Break eggs into a mixing bowl, add the sugar and corn starch, and whip together. In a saucepan, combine the milk, cream, and chocolate. Place on low heat until the chocolate melts. Add egg mixture into saucepan and whisk gently over medium heat until pudding comes to a gentle boil. Keep whisking until cream thickens a bit.

Carefully pour the mixture into martini or wine glasses, or small serving dishes, and refrigerate. When serving, garnish with whipped cream and one Pirouette cookie per glass.

Serves 4–6.

Adapted from a recipe by La Petite Maison in Waterville, NY.

Joanne's Old-Fashioned Egg Custard

This may seem like a dainty for Victorian ladies, but your co-author can tell you he got hooked on this during his years playing football, when the icy cold, slippery sweet wetness of this high-protein, low-fat dessert seemed to be just what his body was craving. It bakes up a beautiful brown skin on top, and has an interesting shimmery, firm consistency very different from pudding, yogurt, or similar treats.

4 cups milk
5 eggs
½ cup sugar
⅛ teaspoon salt
1 teaspoon vanilla

Preheat oven to 325 degrees.

Heat the milk in a double boiler until it is steaming.

In a bowl, beat the eggs, sugar, and salt together, then add to the milk, stirring constantly. Add the vanilla, and keep the water in the double boiler at a rolling boil. Cook for about 5 minutes, or until a metal spoon dipped into the custard comes out coated.

Pour into a lightly buttered casserole or baking dish with high sides. Set the dish into a pan of water in the oven. Bake for about 1 hour, or until the custard is set in the center. Serve well chilled.

Serves 8–10.

Almond-Butter Brownies

Here's a tasty twist on a favorite old standby. If you like almond flavor, you'll enjoy these. Should you have trouble locating almond butter, see Nut Butters in our Resources section.

2 eggs
1 cup sugar
1 teaspoon vanilla
½ teaspoon almond extract
½ teaspoon salt
2 1-ounce squares unsweetened chocolate, melted
½ cup almond butter
¾ cup flour
¾ cup roasted almonds, chopped
Handful (to taste) chocolate chips

Preheat oven to 325 degrees.

Lightly beat eggs. Stir in sugar, vanilla, almond extract, and salt. Blend in melted chocolate and almond butter. Stir in flour, almonds, and chocolate chips. Do not beat batter at any time.

Spread batter into a greased 9-inch pan. Bake for about 40 minutes. Let cool in pan, then cut into squares.

Makes 12 brownies.

Real Butterscotch Pudding

We admit: until the chef at Veraisons Restaurant sent this to us, our experience with butterscotch pudding was pretty much limited to the instant packages we used to stir milk into as kids. So we weren't expecting much. We should have known better—this pudding uses real butter and real scotch, plus plenty of milk and cream. And it is just divine. This will obliterate the memory of those sickly sweet concoctions of your youth!

1 cup milk, plus an additional 1 Tablespoon later

½ cup heavy cream

½ cup brown sugar

2 egg yolks

2 Tablespoons cornstarch

¼ teaspoon vanilla extract

1 Tablespoon whiskey

¼ teaspoon salt

3 Tablespoons butter

In a medium-size saucepan bring the cup of milk, heavy cream, and brown sugar to a simmer.

In a small bowl, add 2 tablespoons of the hot liquid to the egg yolks, and whip together to bring the eggs to room temperature. Add mixture to the pan on the stove.

Next, in a medium bowl mix the remaining tablespoon of milk with the cornstarch, then add the contents from the stove, along with the vanilla, whiskey, and salt. Stir together and return to pan.

Bring back to a simmer while whisking. Once the mixture is thick, whisk in the butter.

Pour into a serving bowl or individual serving glasses and chill for about 3 hours. (Place plastic wrap directly on the pudding so a skin does not form.)

Serves 4–6.

Adapted from a recipe by Veraisons Restaurant in Dundee, NY.

Peanut Butter Mousse

This is a light and fluffy, though very rich, dessert. It's best made in advance and served fully chilled. We intend to test this recipe some day with almond and cashew butters, just to compare.

> 1 cup heavy cream
> ½ teaspoon vanilla
> ¾ cup powdered sugar, divided
> 3 egg whites
> ¼ teaspoon cream of tartar
> ⅜ cup peanut butter

Put the heavy cream, vanilla, and about half of the powdered sugar in a small mixing bowl and beat on high speed until it forms stiff peaks. Put aside in fridge.

Place the egg whites in a medium-size mixing bowl and beat until they froth up to about twice their original volume. Add the cream of tartar and the remainder of the powdered sugar. Resume beating on high speed until the egg whites form peaks.

Place the peanut butter in a large mixing bowl and add about ⅓ of the whipped egg whites. Gently fold them together with a large spatula.

Then add ⅓ of the whipped cream to the mixture and gently fold that together. Continue alternating between the egg whites and the whipped cream until all ingredients are gently but thoroughly folded together.

Spoon small portions into stemmed serving glasses or small cups or dishes, and chill for at least an hour or two. (If you prefer, you can chill the entire bowlful and dip portions later, but it will take longer to chill, and the servings will be messier.)

Serves 6–8.

Adapted from a recipe by Rosalie's Cucina in Skaneateles, NY.

Almond Lace Cups

Beautiful and delicate, these will wow any dinner guests you want to impress. The dough is simple to put together. The tricky part is baking them so that they are just the right size, making sure they don't run together on the sheet as they cook, and lifting them carefully from the tray. It may take a bit of practice, but the directions below will guide you through. And it's worth it!

1 cup sugar
1 cup butter
⅞ cup corn syrup
1 cup flour
1 cup sliced or slivered almonds

Preheat oven to 350 degrees. In a medium-size bowl, cream sugar and butter together with an electric beater, then add corn syrup until combined. Mix in flour. Then fold in almonds with a spatula.

Line several pans or cookie sheets with parchment paper or a nonstick silicone baking mat (e.g. Silpat) if you have one. (Do not skip this step—these cookies are so thin and delicate, they will stick even to a greased pan.)

Scoop rounded teaspoons of dough (literally just one teaspoon) onto the pans. There should be only 3 or 4 of these small scoops per cookie sheet, as they will spread out a lot as they bake.

Sweets

Bake for 9 to 11 minutes, until golden brown. Cool slightly (1 to 2 minutes), then carefully peel them off the paper or Silpat with your hands or a metal spatula.

Place the soft, warm circles over small upside-down drinking glasses or coffee cups to finish cooling. They will sag around the glasses and harden in a bowl-like shape.

Fill the hardened shell with ice cream or sorbet.

This recipe will make numerous cups, depending on how large you make them. You may want to make just a few at a time, and store leftover dough in the freezer or fridge for later use.

Adapted from a recipe by Arad Evans Inn in Fayetteville, NY.

Mary's Chocolate Sauce

For years, this was scrawled in big looping letters inside the cover of an old cookbook, where we knew right where to find it whenever we had a nighttime craving for vanilla ice cream with hot fudge sauce.

This takes no more than 15 minutes to make and you likely have all of the ingredients sitting in your pantry. It blows out of the water any chocolate sauce you can buy in a bottle, and it stores very well in the fridge. Just make sure to reheat it slowly in the microwave or in a double boiler so the chocolate does not burn.

¼ cup butter
3 squares unsweetened baking chocolate
1 5 oz. can evaporated milk
1 cup sugar
A dash of vanilla

In a double boiler, melt the butter and chocolate. Once liquid, add the milk and sugar. Stir regularly until the sauce becomes slightly thick. You can tell the sauce is done if you pour a drop into a glass of cold water and it balls up. If it disperses in the water instead, it needs a few more minutes.

When the sauce is done, stir in the vanilla.

Serve over vanilla ice cream. If you find yourself starting to take dips right out of the container in the fridge, seek professional counseling.

Makes approximately 2 cups.

Ice-Age Wine

The very first winery in the United States was established in the Finger Lakes in about 1836. It wasn't until New York State lifted bothersome legal constraints in the 1980s that artisan winemaking really began to take off in the area. From just a handful, the number of regional winemakers has exploded to more than 130—and as a group they are renowned for being especially innovative, striving, and cooperative in sharing breakthroughs and expertise. The quality of their output has thus risen even faster than the exploding number of local producers.

Cold winters and a relatively short growing season were once thought to make high-quality wine impossible in the Northeast, but the geology of the Finger Lakes offers special advantages which have turned New York into the nation's number two grape grower, behind only California. Throughout the area, shale lies just below the surface, along with outcroppings of limestone. Both of these contribute to the mineral crispness of wine.

When the last of the glaciers retreated from central New York about 10,000 years ago, their meltwater gouged deep V-shaped grooves which became the Finger Lakes. With up to 600 feet of water depth, these lakes serve as temperature reservoirs—reducing peak summer heat that can make wine grapes insipid, holding warmth through the fall, and moderating the early freeze cycle in the spring. Research shows that the "lake effect" can raise minimum winter temperatures along

the lake by more than five degrees, and keep the same vineyards at least two degrees cooler during the summer dog days.

The steep hillsides along the lakes also provide "air drainage." This both reduces the bite of frost and discourages the fungal growth that is the bane of grape growing.

The French use the term *terroir* to encapsulate the delicate mix of soil, weather, mineral, light, and other factors that go into great vintages. Thanks to its ancient Ice Age legacy, and the burgeoning savvy of local growers and winemakers, the Finger Lakes region is turning into one of the world's finest creators of cool-weather wines like Riesling. The fruity, crisp, highly expressive Finger Lakes versions are increasingly celebrated by international critics as equals to august Rhine and Mosel vintages.

And where there is great wine, there will always be great food.

Orange-Riesling Sorbet

This unusual wine sorbet is refreshing and tangy, with lots of rich orange flavor and a nice undercurrent of Riesling. This recipe is adapted from a formulation by the Cayuga Lake Creamery, a delightful Finger Lakes ice cream shop that collaborates with local chefs and wineries to create interesting wine sorbets and ice creams.

> ¾ cup sugar
>
> 1 cup hot water
>
> 3 cups orange juice with lots of pulp
>
> Zest of 1 large orange
>
> 1¾ cups semi-dry Riesling wine
>
> ½ Tablespoon Triple Sec liqueur (Grand Marnier,
>   Courvoisier, etc.—if you want only this small amount,
>   most liquor stores can sell you an "airline-size" bottle)

Stir sugar into hot water until dissolved. Then pour all ingredients into a home ice-cream maker.

Because of the wine, this will not freeze as fast or as hard in your maker as some sorbets. If you want to serve it right away, it may be soft, so to prevent fast melting present it in bowls you've chilled in the freezer. Or pack it into a tub with a tight sealing lid and place in the freezer, where it will freeze solid.

Makes 1½ quarts.

Purple Power

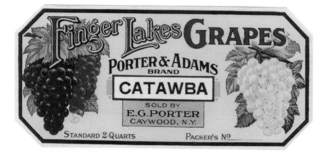

More than 2,000 cultivars of grapes grow in America, but our most famous native variety (and one of only a handful of popular fruits native to North America) is the Concord. Ever since Thomas Welch set up shop in the Finger Lakes, Upstate New York has been the largest Concord-growing region in the world, and the source of most of our drinking juice.

In the past few years, researchers have discovered that juice made from Concord and other American grapes is a powerfully healthy food. The antioxidants concentrated in their purple skins (as well as in some wine grapes, and a few other deep-blue fruits and vegetables) have powerfully wholesome metabolic, heart, cognitive, and anti-cancer effects. These plants synthesize inside their own cells natural antibiotics (like resveratrol) that fight off funguses and other attackers.

Grape juice concentrates these compounds. An eight-ounce glass contains the essence of about 40 grapes. That makes it the equivalent of two USDA fruit servings. And thanks to the special antioxidant power of the polyphenols in grapes like Concords, purple grape juice is an even more significant source of good health than fruits and vegetables of other colors.

Our Resources list includes our favorite New York growers cooperative, which ships a convenient Concord juice concentrate (non-frozen) anywhere in the country. (The same co-op also sells a sour-cherry concentrate that has many of the same healthy benefits of Concord juice, plus a natural anti-inflammatory that aids joint health.) They also sell an organic concentrate if that's important to you. Another Finger Lakes vendor called Glendale Farms sells a special juice blended from grapes of complementary flavors—Concord, Catawba, Delaware, Niagara, and Cayuga.

Should you ever tire of straight grape juice, try mixing it half and half with iced tea. Or fizzing it up with club soda. We also like to add a dollop of the sour cherry concentrate to our grape juice, for extra piquancy and flavor.

If you want to sample an unusual Finger Lakes specialty, try a Grape Pie. The simplest way to make one—the only way when outside the short season when Concords are ripe—is to buy concentrated grape purée from a grower such as the co-op listed in our Resources section under Concord Grapes, then follow the very easy recipe on the jar. If you're not feeling frisky enough to make your own pie, the next best thing is to buy a grape pie (or one of her other 24 varieties!) at Monica's Pies in Naples, New York. (Again, see Resources.) Her clan bakes and sells upwards of 15,000 pies annually, so consider this local icon taste-tested.

Incidentally, when Cornell fruit scientist Dr. Leroy Lawrence started making pioneering measurements of resveratrol content, he found "extraordinarily" high levels of the healthy compound in harvests specifically from the Finger Lakes—fully four times the typical level. It appears that the cold weather and other local qualities, which make the vines work harder, thus producing fruit that's extra tasty, also result in extra-high levels of health-protecting compounds.

Raspberry Red-Wine Sorbet

Another unusual wine sorbet with real raspberry tang and a nice wine secondary taste. Note that this is not smooth and processed, but country-style chunky, with lots of raspberry pulp and seeds.

⅔ cup sugar
¼ cup hot water
3 cups fresh raspberries
1¼ cups red wine
⅔ cup heavy cream
1 Tablespoon lemon or lime
  juice

Stir the sugar into the hot water to mostly melt it. Mash the raspberries up a bit with a large fork or spoon. Mix all ingredients and freeze in a home ice-cream maker.

Because of the wine, this will not freeze as fast or as hard in your maker as some sorbets. If you want to serve it right away, it may be soft, so to prevent fast melting present it in bowls you've chilled in the freezer. Or pack it into a tub with a tight sealing lid and place in the freezer, where it will freeze solid.

Makes 1 quart.

Grape Ice Cream

You've probably never eaten, or even seen, grape ice cream—especially with wine as an ingredient—but this is a simple and delicious treat with a beautiful purple lilac color.

> 2 cups Concord grape juice
> ⅓ cup sugar
> 1 cup milk
> 1 teaspoon lemon or lime juice
> ½ cup white or rosé wine
> 1 cup cream (light cream or heavy whipping cream, depending on how rich you like your ice creams)

Heat the grape juice slightly in microwave or on stove top so that the sugar dissolves when you stir it in. Then mix in all other ingredients. Freeze in a home ice-cream maker.

Because of the wine, this will not freeze as fast or as hard in your maker as some ice creams. If you want to serve it right away, it may be soft, so to prevent fast melting present it in bowls you've chilled in the freezer. Or pack it into a tub with a tight-sealing lid and place in the freezer, where it will freeze solid.

Makes 1 quart.

Maple Mousse with Blueberries

6 egg yolks
¾ cup maple syrup
1 pint heavy cream
1 pint blueberries, divided

Beat egg yolks and syrup together and heat on stove top, continuing to beat until slightly thickened. Chill for a couple hours. Then beat heavy cream until it forms stiff peaks, fold in the egg/maple mixture and half of the blueberries, and serve with the rest of the blueberries sprinkled on top of the servings.

Serves 8.

Maple Gingerbread

2 cups flour
1 teaspoon ginger
½ teaspoon salt
1 teaspoon baking soda
1 teaspoon cinnamon
1 cup maple syrup
1 egg, beaten
1 cup sour cream
Whipped cream

Preheat oven to 350 degrees.

Combine dry ingredients thoroughly. In a mixing bowl, fold together maple syrup, beaten egg, and sour cream; then add dry ingredients. Bake in a 10-inch round greased pan until fork emerges cleanly from center (about 30 minutes). Serve with a dousing of maple syrup and a dollop of whipped cream.

Serves 8.

Chocolate Sauerkraut Cake

In addition to the favorite savory applications mentioned in our Salads & Side Dishes section, Finger Lakers are fond of some unusual uses of sauerkraut. One improbable recipe is this Chocolate Sauerkraut Cake. (If you think your eaters might be squeamish, you can call it Chocolate Mystery Cake.) The sauerkraut adds a texture similar to shredded coconut.

¾ cup sauerkraut—rinsed lightly, drained,
    chopped fine, and packed loosely into measure
2 cups flour
1 teaspoon baking soda
1 teaspoon baking powder
½ teaspoon salt
⅔ cup unsweetened cocoa powder
1½ cups sugar
⅔ cup butter, melted
1 teaspoon vanilla extract
3 eggs
1 cup yogurt or buttermilk

Preheat oven to 350 degrees.

Grease one 9" x 13" baking pan.

Prep sauerkraut as described above and set aside. Mix flour, baking soda, baking powder, salt, and cocoa together and set aside. In a mixing bowl, beat sugar, butter, and vanilla together, then add eggs—folding them in one at a time with electric mixer. With mixer on slow speed, add in dry ingredients and yogurt or buttermilk in 2 to 3 alternating pours. Once mixture is smooth, fold in sauerkraut with large spoon. Pour into greased baking pan, and bake for 30 minutes, or until inserted toothpick comes out clean. Frost with your favorite vanilla or chocolate icing once cool.

Makes one 9" x 13" cake.

Contributing Finger Lakes Restaurants

Our sincere thanks to the chefs and owners of these wonderfully inventive New York State eateries for sharing their recipes and stories with our readers.

Arad Evans Inn
Fayetteville
315.637.2020
aradevansinn.com

The Belhurst
Geneva
315.781.0201
belhurst.com

Castel Grisch
Watkins Glen
607.535.9614
castelgrisch.com

Cayuga Lake Creamery
Interlaken
607.532.9492
cayugalakecreamery.com

Cobblestone Restaurant
Geneva
315.789.8498
cobblestonegeneva.com

Dano's Heuriger on Seneca
Lodi
607.582.7555
danosonseneca.com

Dinosaur Bar-B-Que
Syracuse and Rochester
315.476.4937 Syr
585.325.9127 Roch
dinosaurbarbque.com

Hazelnut Kitchen
Trumansburg
607.387.4433
hazelnutkitchen.com

Just a Taste Wine & Tapas Bar
Ithaca
607.277.9463
just-a-taste.com

La Petite Maison
Waterville
315.841.8030

Maxie's Supper Club
Ithaca
607.272.4136
maxies.com

Mirbeau Inn
Skaneateles
315.685.5006
mirbeau.com

Moosewood Restaurant
Ithaca
607.273.9610
moosewoodrestaurant.com

Next Door Bar & Grill
Pittsford
585.249.4575
nextdoorbarandgrill.com

Ports Cafe
Geneva
315.789.2020
portscafe.com

Red Newt Bistro
Hector
607.546.4100
rednewt.com

The Restaurant at Knapp Vineyards
Romulus
800.869.9271
knappwine.com/Vineyard-Restaurant

Rosalie's Cucina
Skaneateles
315.685.2200
rosaliescucina.com

Simply Red Bistro
Ovid
607.532.9401
simplyredbistro.com

Stonecat Cafe
Hector
607.546.5000
stonecatcafe.com

Suzanne Fine Regional Cuisine
Lodi
607.582.7545
suzannefrc.com

Veraisons Restaurant
Dundee
800.243.5513
glenora.com/restaurant

Contributing Finger Lakes Restaurants

Village Tavern
Hammondsport
607.569.2528
villagetaverninn.com

Zabroso Restaurant
Oneida
315.363.3360
zabrosorestaurant.com

Contributing Finger Lakes Restaurants

Resources

Apples

Apples don't ship well, so to crunch some of the truly superb fruit available in the Finger Lakes region, you'll need to visit. If you do, here are a few treasures from among the many excellent orchards of Upstate New York:

Beak and Skiff (celebrating their 100th year in 2012)
  beakandskiff.com

Cornell Orchards
  hort.cals.cornell.edu/cals/hort/about/cornell_orchards.cfm

Littletree Orchards
  littletree-orchards.com

Red Jacket
  redjacketorchards.com

If you live near New York, here is a great Web tool provided by the state apple growers' association that will help you find an orchard that grows whatever apple variety you desire.
  nyapplecountry.com/findvariety.php

There are also cideries by the dozen in the area, some of which offer hard as well as fresh cider. Some, Beak and Skiff for one, even make apple wines and vodka. So do a little exploring and then crunch and sip away!

Buckwheat

The Birkett Mills
In operation since 1797, they still occupy their old mill in the heart of a small village, and operate as the world's largest manufacturer of buckwheat products. You can purchase buckwheat flour for crepes, kasha, pancake mix; even seed to grow your own plants; or hulls for stuffing into pillows.
  thebirkettmills.com/shop/

Concord Grapes

(juice, grape-seed oil & grape pie filling)

Growers' Co-op
Owned by about 150 Upstate New York grape growers, these products come right
from the producers. We order several bottles of the concentrate, which will make
many gallons of healthful juice. They also offer a tangy tart-cherry juice concentrate
which we sometimes mix into the grape juice for variety. In addition, they sell grape-
seed oil, which is an alternative to olive oil (see Artisan Oils on page 50), and a
concord-grape purée—which provides a simple and year-round way to make that
unusual Finger Lakes signature: a grape pie! (Directions are on the purée container.)
    concordgrapejuice.com

Finger Lakes Cheese

This site gives a roster of New York cheese makers provided by the New York State
Farmstead and Artisan Cheese Makers Guild, some of whom ship.
    nyfarmcheese.org/cheesemakers.asp

This is a tighter listing of Finger Lakes cheese makers.
    ilovethefingerlakes.com/basics/agriculture-cheesemakers.htm

Particularly popular local goat cheeses are available here.
    livelyrun.com

An unusual kefir cheese is made here.
    fingerlakesdextercreamery.com/buyingcheese.html

Fruit Butters

Blackman Homestead Farm
They sell unusual, tasty fruit butters. Apple Cinnamon, Apple Walnut, Cherry
Almond, Pear and Port, Pear Vanilla, and Pumpkin Maple butters can be eaten
on toast or paired with cheeses, dolloped on meats, or used as dessert toppings.
The Blackman family also sells a Concord-grape pie filling of the type described in
Purple Power on pages 178.
    blackmanhomesteadfarm.com/stores.html

Fruit Juices

Red Jacket Orchards
This company offers a variety of juices, including an acclaimed Sour Cherry Stomp, and a Juice of the Month Club.

    redjacketorchards.com

German Frankfurters

Liehs & Steigerwald
If you're ever in Syracuse, New York, this little shop is the greatest German sausage maker in the business.

    liehsandsteigerwald.com

Hofmann Sausage
If you're seeking central New York–style franks, Coneys, brats, kielbasa, and other sausages from afar, you'll find two options at the website below—a retail store locator covering many parts of the country, and online ordering if you want them delivered to your door:

    hofmannsausage.com

Grape Pie

If you're in Naples, New York, you can purchase a Finger Lakes grape pie at Monica's. Sorry, they don't ship anymore.

    monicaspies.com

Hens

If you're researching keeping laying hens in the backyard, here are excellent resources for informing yourself, neighbors, and government officials about the merits.

    backyardchickens.com/a/how-we-changed-our-laws

    scribd.com/doc/16509728/Changing-Your-Citys-Chicken-Laws

Honey

Waid Apiaries
This Interlaken, New York, beekeeper makes fine varietal honeys like Apple Blossom, Basswood, Buckwheat, Goldenrod, and Strawberry that vary widely in color and flavor. They also sell creamed and combed honey, beeswax candles, and other related products. And they ship!
607.532.4391
waidshoney@fltg.net

Find your own local honey producers at honeylocator.com.

The killer-bee honey described in Fruit and Nut Butters on pages 40-41 can be ordered only in cases of 12 one-pound jars at the maker's site, but you can purchase single jars here.
plummarket.com/wine/once-again-killer-bee-honey-1lb.html

Maple Cinnamon Bread

Abbey of the Genesee Trappist Monastery
This monastery makes a variety of breads, but we love their amazing Maple Cinnamon bread, made with real maple syrup. We've never had anything quite like it. The best deal is six loaves (they freeze beautifully) for $19.95.
shop.monksbread.com/

Maple Syrup

To find a nearby provider of New York State maple syrup, check out this website.
nysmaple.com

Mushrooms

Blue Oyster Cultivation
A family-owned gourmet mushroom farm located in Ithaca, New York. Online they sell online New York dried mushrooms (chanterelles or reishi), as well as Finger Lakes mushroom tea, and even a kit which allows you to grow your own oyster mushrooms at home.
blueoystercultivation.com

Nut Butters

Once Again

This employee-owned company offers a wide variety of peanut, almond, and cashew butters, plus tahini and sunflower-seed butters, and honeys—including killer-bee honey. To find a retail store in your area:

onceagainnutbutter.com/Store_Locator.html

Their own online store sells mostly by the case. For single-jar sales, a handier vendor is the nearby Abbey of the Genesee Trappist Monastery (mentioned earlier in this section for their wonderful maple cinnamon bread). The monastery sells their own bread online plus the products of other local food makers like Once Again.

shop.monksbread.com/

You can also buy jars of Once Again products on Amazon.com.

Stoneground Grains, Artisan Flours, Baking Mixes

Farmer Ground Flour

For a list of stores selling Farmer Ground flours in New York visit their website.

farmergroundflour.com

To buy their flour online go here.

cporganics.com/store/organic-flour

New Hope Mills

This august old company offers lots of baking mixes and grain products.

newhopemills.com

North Country Farms

Though their online shopping cart is not yet in operation, this miller of superb flours promises one soon.

ncfarms.net

Squash-Seed Oils

Stony Brook Wholehearted Foods

Highly flavorful alternatives to olive oil are made from the seeds of butternut, delicata, acorn, and buttercup squash, as well as pumpkin seeds. They sell directly online at their website. And see a list of retail stores in twenty states that carry their oils.

wholeheartedfoods.com

Verjus

Pronounced "vair-ZHOO" and meaning literally "green juice," verjus is the sweet/tart mildly acidic liquid pressed from unripe (green) wine grapes. It makes a great addition to sauces, salad dressings, and other cooking where you might otherwise use red-wine vinegar or lemon juice. On page 66, see our Apricot Black Bean & Verjus Salsa recipe that relies on verjus for its tang.

Red Newt Cellars
Verjooz brand verjus made by Red Newt Cellars, an excellent Finger Lakes winery, can be purchased on the winery's website.
   rednewt.com

Wines from the Finger Lakes

Here is a site maintained by a coalition of vineyards to introduce you generally to Finger Lakes wines: fingerlakeswinealliance.com

If you're in the vicinity of Ithaca, New York, the Finger Lakes Wine Center is a good place to taste a range of Finger Lakes vintages and get oriented on what the region's wineries offer: FingerLakesWineCenter.org

Each of the major lakes offers its own wine trail, which links a half-dozen to two dozen wineries in an easy-to-tour group. You can stop at the wineries that interest you and taste for very reasonable fees ($5 or under). There are opportunities to eat well along the way. And the scenery is lovely.
   cayugawinetrail.com
   senecalakewine.com
   keukawinetrail.com

Once you begin to develop favorites, nearly all of the 130+ Finger Lakes wineries have their own websites, many able to ship bottles. To get you started, here is an entirely subjective list of a few of our personal favorites:

Anthony Road Wine Company
   anthonyroadwine.com

Chateau Lafayette Reneau
   clrwine.com

Dr. Frank's Vinifera Wine Cellars
  drfrankwines.com

Hermann J. Wiemer Vineyard
  wiemer.com

Lamoreaux Landing Wine Cellars
  lamoreauxwine.com

Ravines Wine Cellars
  ravineswine.com

Red Newt Cellars
  rednewt.com

The first "wine of the month" organization focused exclusively on Finger Lakes Wine is coming soon. As soon as they complete their groundwork, three choices of membership will be available: fingerlakeswinesociety.com

Yogurts

As described on page 124, two skyrocketing central New York producers—Chobani and Fage—have pioneered today's red-hot new market for Greek yogurts.

To find stores near you selling Chobani, go here.
  chobani.com/products/where

To find stores near you selling Fage, go here.
  fageusa.com/store-locator

As of this writing, the fascinating vegetable and spicy aMaMa yogurts—Vege'Yo' and SpicyYo'—are available in specialty stores only in the Finger Lakes region. For more information see amama.com.

Creators

Kate Harvey lives in New York City, where she divides her time among writing, performing and teaching classical music, and cooking. She did most of the magic in our test kitchen. Kate has a master's in piano performance, and majored in piano and American Studies at Notre Dame. She has been a journalist, an editorial assistant, and even composed music. This is her first book. Kate's recent wedding took place in the Finger Lakes. Of course, local food and Riesling were served at the reception!

Karl Zinsmeister has written for magazines and newspapers including *The Atlantic* and *The Wall Street Journal.* He and his wife, Ann, produced a PBS film aired nationally in 2007. He has written several books, including a memoir; two Iraq War journals written as an embedded reporter; and even a Marvel comic book. He has been a magazine editor-in-chief, an executive at the historic Stickley company, and currently serves at The Philanthropy Roundtable. In previous lives, Karl was an aide to Daniel Patrick Moynihan in the U.S. Senate, and was chief domestic policy advisor to George W. Bush in the White House. An avid outdoorsman, gardener, and renovator of old houses, he currently lives on a houseboat in Washington, D.C., and owns an 1898 Victorian in Cazenovia, NY.

Photographer **Noah Zinsmeister** is a student at Columbia University. His work has been featured in art exhibits, magazines, newspapers, and on the Internet; his camera of choice is a Canon. This is his first book. During production, he ate more than his fair share of the dishes as they emerged from oven and skillet—*usually* after photographing them. In his free time, Noah is a political enthusiast, enjoys creating and appreciating music, plays tennis, and skis.

Noah and Kate are sixth-generation residents of the Finger Lakes. Karl is their father.

Index